The Shuttleworth Collection

The Shuttleworth Collection

David Ogilvy

The official guide

An Airlife publication in the Shuttleworth Series.

Airlife

England

©
1982
David Ogilvy
Jocelyn Millard
Chris Morris

First Published in 1982
by Airlife Publishing Ltd.

ISBN 0 906393 18 3

Airlife Publishing Ltd.
7 St. John's Hill, Shrewsbury, England.

Printed by Livesey Limited, Shrewsbury, England.

Contents

Introduction — and an appreciation

This new guide to the Shuttleworth Collection takes on an entirely fresh format and, unlike its predecessor, relates mainly to the aeroplanes and the items that have direct aviation connections. The many other examples of historic transport, such as motor cars, bicycles, motorcycles, fire engines and horse-drawn vehicles receive only brief reference as they are covered in a series of specialised booklets.

This is an entirely new publication, but the origin of the Shuttleworth guide dates from 1964, when Wing Commander T. E. Guttery, then the Collection's Honorary Librarian and Archivist, produced the first edition. Subsequently he updated the guide to keep pace with progress and his final much-enlarged version appeared in both hard-back and paper-back forms as recently as 1976. Wing Commander Guttery's aviation experience started in 1912 when he joined the Royal Flying Corps in the year of its formation, but he died in 1978.

There can be no substitute for sixty-six years of experience in a broad band of aviation activity and to endeavour to follow the pattern set by the original author could lead only to an editorial mishap. So I have begun afresh with a lead-in about the background to the Collection; followed by a chapter on early development of the flying machine, using the Shuttleworth exhibits as bases for comparison. After that, aircraft development and the related types are grouped into the 1914-18 war with the subsequent periods divided into separate chapters covering civil and military designs. Later follow descriptions of the various aeronautica in the Collection: aero engines, propellers, relics of the era of airships and balloons and many others. Later chapters describe the restoration tasks carried out in the workshops and the general differences in the handling qualities of ancient and modern flying machines.

The aircraft in the Shuttleworth Collection are priceless; many are the World's sole survivors of their types. Their importance in history increases when each is considered not only as itself, but as a significant stage in the whole story that leads to aviation as we know it today. But it has happened during this century; there are people alive now who were born before the first aeroplane climbed from the ground under its own power. That adds a very personal 'living' element to the scene and makes the progress so interesting and, perhaps, more easily understandable.

There is one key to the whole Shuttleworth story: the aeroplanes fly. For that, and for the overall existence of the Collection, we must remember the aims and activities of the founder, Richard Ormonde Shuttleworth, who began in 1928 and had the foresight to make everything work. At first he acquired veteran motor cars, but soon he extended to aircraft and, in the thirties, he obtained the earliest of the flying machines; today these form the base on which the post-war expansion has been built. In recent years no one could have obtained a Bleriot of 1909, a Deperdussin that is only a year younger or a 1912 Blackburn, but Richard Shuttleworth discovered all these and others when few people considered it to be 'fashionable' to do so; almost certainly if he had failed to find them they would have disappeared many years ago.

Various people have helped in the preparation of this Shuttleworth story. Jocelyn Millard, the Collection's guide and information officer, has cross-checked many of the facts and has written the sections devoted to the static exhibits; Chris Morris, the chief inspector, has added some technical detail; Michael Vines, David Davies (both of Air Portraits), John Hoad and Peter Green have provided the pictures; and the Collection's secretarial staff have unscrambled my scrawl and converted it into usable matter. Please remember the parts that they — and others — have played in making this into what I hope is both a readable and an accurate description of a unique organisation.

Finally, I would like to thank Wing Commander Oliver Wells, an Aviation Trustee and Chairman of the Executive Committee, and Wing Commander R. F. (Dick) Martin, who is the Collection's senior and most experienced pilot, for plodding patiently through the drafts and adding some useful suggestions which I have been pleased to incorporate.

DAVID OGILVY
Summer 1982

Chapter 1
Origins of the Shuttleworth Collection

A Shuttleworth connection with aeroplanes dates further back than many people realise, for the ancestral firm of Clayton and Shuttleworth had operated factories in Lincoln since 1842 and these produced aircraft during World War 1. Primarily a heavy engineering company, making steam traction and ploughing engines, the firm's skills and resources were turned to the manufacture of Sopwith Camels, more than 500 of which were built between 1917 and 1919. These were delivered mainly to the Royal Naval Air Service, but some went to Belgium, where one remains in existence today. The famous German ace Captain (Baron) Manfred von Richtofen was shot down and killed by a Shuttleworth-built Camel B7270.

An entry into the production of heavier aircraft coincided with construction of a new (third) factory alongside the River Witham. Here the company built 46 of the large Handley Page 0/400 twin-engine bombers (powered by Rolls-Royce Eagles) and as these were too massive to transport by surface to an aerodrome, they were flown from a small field adjacent to the works. They were very lightly loaded for the short flight to a nearby Aircraft Acceptance Park. In 1916, though, before any complete aeroplanes were built, Clayton and Shuttleworth had made tail stabilisers and gondola parts for Submarine Scout airships that were used by the Admiralty on coastal patrol duties.

In the twenties and thirties relatively few people thought about obtaining early cars or aeroplanes, but Richard Shuttleworth had the foresight and determination to obtain some exceptionally worthwhile examples of both. The fortunate son of a wealthy land-owning family, he had access to the space necessary to build workshops, a hangar and the small grass aerodrome at Old Warden, near Biggleswade in Bedfordshire. Perhaps the aerodrome is one of the most significant aspects of it all, for Richard was no museum man; he obtained items to make them work. His cars participated in the annual Brighton runs and his aeroplanes flew regularly at displays.

In the eighties, the name Shuttleworth is known to many thousands of people all over the world, but this is not surprising as the Collection is well past the half-way point in its first century of existence. In September 1978 a special fiftieth anniversary pageant brought every airworthy aeroplane and every runnable road vehicle into action, to enable discerning visitors to see the scale of the operation that had been established. Although a very special event, this pageant was one of the regular series of displays held at Old Warden throughout the summer months. But it was not always like this, for there has been a steady growth since 1928, when Richard Shuttleworth began his collecting activites by acquiring a (then) thirty-years-old Panhard Levassor motor car. That car remains a key exhibit today and in recent years has been restored (again) to excellent running order.

Although, through the Collection, Richard Shuttleworth is remembered mainly for his avid acquisition of historic aircraft and vehicles, we must not overlook his activities as a successful racing driver; he based his racing operations on the famous track at Brooklands, where he had his original workshop, but he participated in events in many parts of the continent and even as far afield as South Africa, where on 1st January 1936 he had a serious accident that ended his racing career. It was at Brooklands, significantly, that in 1932 he bought his first aeroplane; not then a collector's piece, but a four-years-old de Havilland Moth that he used as his regular fly-about, particularly for journeys between there and Old Warden. With the passage of time, that Moth has gained in rarity value to become one of the leading items on show; as evidence of the years that have gone, by 1982 this Moth had been based at Old Warden for half a century and had lived on one aerodrome for longer than any other aeroplane in the history of aviation!

In addition to collecting and racing, Richard Shuttleworth founded the Warden Aviation Company, based at Heston and equipped with three Desoutters and a DH Dragon for charter flying; the Dragon was specially modified with a Carden-Ford engine as a generator and the aircraft was fitted with an array of lights for aerial advertising at night. Several companies, including two breweries, placed contracts, but the authorities of the time reacted to unfavourable public opinion and the project was banned almost before it had begun. As a Director of Pobjoy Airmotor and later of the Comper Aircraft Co. Ltd. of Hooton Park, Cheshire, Richard flew a diminutive single-seat Swift to India on a marketing tour. His aeronautical activities at Old Warden were mainly on the technical side and these were carried out in the name of the Warden Engineering Company, based in the one hangar near the aerodrome gate, above which were his drawing office and associated rooms; today that hangar houses the earliest aeroplanes, which are among the oldest to be seen anywhere in the world, while the upstairs area is the Collection's main office block housing the administrative staff. Early in these proceedings, L. A. Jackson had come from Brooklands to Old Warden as the first engineer; apart from war service in the Royal Air Force, during which he became a Squadron Leader in the Engineering Branch, Tony ('Jacko') Jackson remained with the Collection until he retired as manager in 1966.

All the Old Warden activities stopped on the outbreak of war in 1939; the aircraft, vehicles and supporting items were stored wherever space could be found to house them; Richard joined the Royal Air Force to qualify as a Service pilot, but unfortunately he was killed in a flying accident in a Fairey Battle light bomber in 1940. The buildings and aerodromes were used for dismantling, assembling and flight-testing of various light types then in RAF

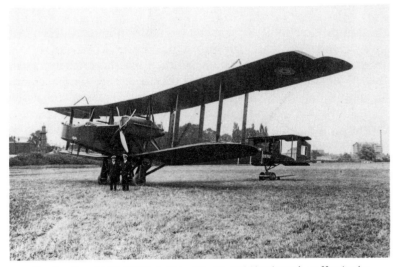

Handley Page 0/400 D9702, built by Clayton and Shuttleworth, at Huntingdon Aerodrome in August, 1918.

13

use; these included Proctors, Harvards and Magisters, on which extensive maintenance and repair work was carried out on the airframe components in premises in Biggleswade owned by Owen Godfrey Ltd. and Mantles Garages Ltd. The activities at the airfield, which included engine overhaul, were carried out through staff employed by Shrager Brothers Ltd., who formed their own Home Guard platoon to protect the premises. A second hangar and several smaller buildings were erected during this time and the maintenance flight testing was carried out by a Service pilot detached from the nearby Royal Air Force station at Henlow.

After the war Mrs Dorothy Shuttleworth, O.B.E., founded and endowed the Richard Ormonde Shuttleworth Remembrance Trust in her son's memory, to provide an educational centre "for the teaching of the science and practice of aviation and of afforestation and agriculture." The last two of these are handled by the nearby Shuttleworth Agricultural College, in the original family house, while the laid-down aims on the aeronautical side are carried out at the aerodrome. Although not now trading as commercial organisations, Richard's two firms have been merged into the Warden Aviation and Engineering Company, which is used as the operating name for the Collection, the aerodrome and the workshops.

The educational aspect of the Collection's activities must not be overlooked; students of all ages and from all over the world use Old Warden for their historical studies and researches; many thousands of schoolchildren visit the Collection each year to be given explanatory talks about the background of aviation and transport and to see the products of the past; lectures are given over a wide geographical area to specialist clubs and societies wishing to learn about the early stages of development of the flying machine; and there are numerous Shuttleworth publications to provide a home-learning facility in transport subjects ranging from horse-drawn vehicles and manual fire engines to motor cycles and aero engines.

To support all this is an ever-growing range of working items that are on static view daily and which can be seen in action on special occasions. Much remains to be done, for the Collection is financed from its own gate receipts and shop sales; this calls for a tight working budget, so limitations of space, workshop capacity, availability of the skilled workforce and other enforced constraints must mean that many tasks wait for several years in the queue before they can be tackled. At present the ruling policy lays main stress on restoring and maintaining the most significant historic aeroplanes, with a separate but smaller department giving similar treatment to selected early road vehcies. A point that many people forget is that a working technical object, once restored, needs constant running maintenance, so each completed item presents a permanent work commitment and therefore reduces the capacity available for further restoration.

As the tasks increase in scope and complexity, so must the supporting facilities. In the seventies two new hangars and workshops were built and by 1979 engine and machine shops and bonded stores had been constructed within the existing buildings; in 1980, a new hangar was opened to public viewing to provide space for a significant increase in displayed material. In 1982, though, a departure from previous policy reached fruition, when a new display building was completed especially to house aeroplanes of de Havilland origin. Now, with more space available, extensive effort is being devoted to improving the presentation of the static exhibits.

Within the past decade there have been three physical expansions to the aircraft manoeuvring area of the aerodrome, to provide a capability for operating heavier and faster aircraft, but still retaining the essential timelessness of a smallish all-grass aerodrome in a rural area. The grass surface and availability of

A Tractor built by Clayton and Shuttleworth on aircraft towing duties, probably in 1919.

several take-off and landing directions are critical for the early aircraft, many of which would be unable to operate from today's airfields with single hard runways.

The Collection's normal routine activity should be self-supporting and any small operating surplus is ploughed back for expansion or improvement; however, this cannot cover the costs of the major projects, such as a particularly expensive restoration task or the provision of a new hangar in which to display the exhibits when they have been restored. For such purposes specialised appeals may be launched, while financial help is always welcome; money can be donated for a specific purpose or, more usually, for the overall good of the whole Collection. Help in kind, too, plays its part, with many organisations and individuals providing services free or at drastically reduced prices; only with such constant support from outside can the work be continued at its present encouraging pace.

A way in which many people show their support for the cause is by joining the Shuttleworth Veteran Aeroplane Society; in return, members receive special entry privileges and are kept in contact with plans and progress through regular news circulars. Membership, which spreads well into four figures, includes historians, enthusiasts and other supporters from almost every country in the world. The benefits are mutual.

How does it all function? A Board of Trustees provides the umbrella of policy for the whole Trust, but with the college, several farms, an estate of nearly 6,000 acres, most of Old Warden village and numerous other buildings in ownership and in need of management, there are many problems for the Board to consider; so an Aerodrome Committee, with four Trustees and four others with specialist experience, concerns itself exclusively with activities at the aerodrome and a smaller Executive Committee meets each month to be even closer to the operational pulse. The Aerodrome Committee is chaired by Marshal of the Royal Air Force Sir John Grandy, formerly Chief of the Air Staff and, later, Chief of the Defence Staff.

To keep overheads pruned, the staff members are kept to a practical minimum, but there are countless duties to be performed; aircraft and vehicle restoration and maintenance, library and research work, sales activities, party visits, building and aerodrome maintenance, accounts, promotion and publicity, general administration and heavy daily correspondence, dealing with inquiries and the planning, operation and management of a well-loaded events programme are some. But how many visitors, perhaps, realise that the international promotion/publicity programme with its preparation, printing and circulation occupies one small section of the staff for the bulk of the three darkest winter months each year? Or that when a historic aeroplane is dismantled for full restoration, this may be the start of a task that will take five or more years? Or that the same machine will need extensive reconditioning again about ten years after it emerges for the first time? Or that initial preparations for a large flying display must begin nearly a year ahead of the date of the event?

The Collection is very much alive throughout the year; alive to the changes that are taking place everywhere, but equally aware of the need to retain that special informal dateless atmosphere which means so much to so many; alive in that the items in its care are not static museum exhibits, but working examples of some of the best of the past; alive, too, to the responsibilities that go with that — whether testing a steam car with an 80 years-old boiler, or maintaining or flying the last surviving specimen of a famous historic aeroplane. Although different times of year produce changes in the nature of the work, there is no slack season at Shuttleworth. There is always more than enough to do; and plenty to see.

In this guide I aim to describe the aeroplanes and some of the

Richard Shuttleworth on the move in his Alfa-Romeo

17

associated items in a sequence and a manner that explain the development of the flying machine itself and, to a smaller extent, the progress of aviation. Each main era and, later, each main subject, qualifies for a chapter of its own; either you can work straight through as though reading a novel, or select the sections to suit your own quest for information. The choice, of course, must rest with you as the reader.

Chapter 2
The Early Flying Machine

Although the brothers Wilbur and Orville Wright must take full credit for the first man-carrying powered flights, starting with the famous 'straights' flown at Kittyhawk, North Carolina on 17th December 1903, there were pioneers before them who very nearly made the grade.

Without doubt Sir George Cayley was the person who started aviation in its modern sense. He gained a great knowledge of aerodynamics, even to the extent of proving that on a cambered aerofoil more lift is generated by the reduced pressure on the upper surface than from the increased pressure beneath; from 1804 he was flying machines of various shapes and sizes with equally varying levels of success. The theoretrical knowledge required to produce sustained flight was there, but for about a hundred years the lack of a suitable engine prevented any real achievement in the way of powered flight. There were many imaginative ideas, of which Henson's 'Aerial Steam Carriage' of 1842 became perhaps the best known, but although the design incorporated many novel ideas that bore future fruit for others, it remained only a paper exercise.

Because of problems of power — or lack of it — experiments with gliding played a lead part in the development of flight, particularly over matters of controllability in the air. No one could equal the pioneering efforts of the German Otto Lilienthal, who flew successfully from 1891 onwards; in fact, development has turned a full circle, for he hung beneath his machine, shifting his body and legs to move the centre of gravity and therefore achieving limited manoeuvrability in broadly the manner used today by the modern and rapidly-developing hang glider. To achieve positive control response more rapidly, Lilienthal experimented later with more convential control surfaces, but he

19

was killed in 1896 before he had developed these. Nearer home, the Scotsman Percy Pilcher achieved success with his glider just before the start of this century, but he too died whilst pioneering the principles of flight. Already he had designed and partially built a powered aeroplane and, if he had lived, might have been the first to succeed.

Even before man-lifting gliders flew successfully, many people endeavoured to achieve powered flight with steam engines; early and serious attempts were made by L.P. Frost of Cambridge, who, from 1868 onward, aimed to fly by following the wing-flapping principles of birds. His ornithopters were developed over about eight years and, to take the bird image to its limit, he copied the wing pattern of the crow, scaling up the precise shape and position of each feather; his principle, presumably, was that if it worked for the crow it should do so for man. This steam engine, an Ahrbecker of 5 h.p. (an original specimen of which is on show in the Collection) weighed 110 lbs and failed to produce the energy needed to flap the wings with sufficient power and the project failed. In 1908, though, the Royal Aeronautical Society declared that if the power had been available the Frost ornithopter should have flown successfully.

The petrol engine saw daylight in 1885 on the first motor-carriage (a three-wheeler produced by Benz), followed a year later by Daimler with a four-stroke motor-cycle, but designers' efforts to harness this for the aeroplane were thwarted by heavy weight and low output. Although the Wrights established world fame by their success with the powered Flyer 1, their practical knowledge had been based on four years' experience, firstly with a towed kite in 1899 and afterwards by man-carrying gliders. In practice, the Wrights, deserve credit for much more than their initial achievement in 1903, for a year later they were flying circuits and when Wilbur gave demonstrations in France in 1908 his proof of success and knowledge spurred the Europeans into action. Before then, on this side of the Atlantic, efforts had been only marginally successful and the Wrights were many years ahead. Although most people realise that the Wrights designed their own aircraft, not all appreciate that they designed their own engine and remarkably efficient propellers which rotated in opposite directions and were geared down to rotate at less than engine speed in order to obtain maximum performance. They built a working wind-tunnel in which to test their theories and a recent reproduction of this exists at Old Warden.

In model form the Collection houses specimens of two very early flying machines. One is a large scale model of the original Wright Flyer 1, made especially to complete the Collection's range of exhibits from the birth of powered flight. The second item displays the ideas and constructional methods behind the British Matchless, a design patented in 1909 by Arthur Phillips of Market Drayton in Shropshire, who was a cycle maker. This is unusual because it was one of the earliest 'convertiplanes', in which the propellers could be rotated in pitch to provide power for either vertical or horizontal flight. A motor-cycle engine enabled the original machine to make several successful tethered flights, but development ceased before its intended power unit — a two-stroke air-cooled rotary engine of Mr Phillips' own design — was ready to use. The principle of vertical/horizontal power deflection has been studied at intervals throughout the progress of flight; today's Harrier is the logical outcome.

At this stage we turn our concentration towards the full-size aeroplane, the basic layout of which tended to stabilise over the few years before the first world war, which is treated in a later chapter. Birds are monoplanes, so it is natural for many early designers to have followed suit. There were exceptions, of course, and those who saw the famous film 'Those Magnificent Men in their Flying Machines' may well have a rather imaginative idea of the varieties of ways in which man aimed to take to the air.

We consider that we live in an active do-it-yourself era, but the efforts of the first aviation pioneers place us all in a rather dark shadow. In the very early nineteen hundreds, the unknown elements of flight were almost countless: the precise wing shape and areas needed to obtain the required lift; the thickness of materials needed for the structure, to avoid failure through weakness or through being too heavy to fly; the controls needed to achieve success in all three flight axes; how to transmit power from a heavy, low-energy engine through a propeller (which itself needed to be of practical design) rather than through road wheels; and if the machine should fly, how to manage it in the air.

Often these and the other associated problems were tackled by one man who designed, built and flew the end product, all of which gave early aviation a very important personal touch that tended to remain in the industry until the numerous smaller firms were rolled into progressively reducing numbers of impersonalised units. Today, alas, the net of nationalisation has swept even those into oblivion.

Let us take a broad look at the aeroplane up to 1912. As evidence of the monoplane trend which was particularly strong in Europe, the Collection contains three specimens from that period: two from France and one of British brew. All have their wing loads taken externally, with pylons above the fuselages from which wires are run to attachment points at roughly mid-span to take the landing stresses; from beneath, attached to the undercarriage structure, similar wires run upwards and are attached to the wing undersurfaces to take the flying loads. This arrangement formed the basis on which the braced monoplane became a practical proposition.

Rudders, already with many years of waterborne proving behind them, were an obvious requirement and were brought into use as hinged surfaces from the start; often they formed the sole vertical tail element while some early designers introduced the fixed fin to provide additional directional stability. Logically moveable elevators mounted on fixed horizontal tailplanes were soon the accepted norm, although some machines had elevators only, with no fixed tailplanes; these perhaps, can bear some comparison with many of today's designs with their all-moving horizontal tail surfaces.

It was in lateral control that the pioneers used a method that is wholly foreign to the modern mind. Instead of having hinged ailerons, one of which would move up and the other down as the column was moved sideways, the wing structure itself was built with a flexibility that enabled the equivalent result to be achieved by twisting: this became known as wing-warping. With the wheel turned to the left, effectively the wing on that side would reduce both in incidence and in lift-generating shape towards the tip, while the right wing tip would increase in camber and angle and therefore provide additional lift, producing a rolling motion to the left. Although this method of roll control worked reasonably well, it proved to be imprecise and sometimes unpredictable, so the separate hinged aileron came into its own quite early in the development process.

Some features of the first aeroplanes disappeared from popularity to re-appear many years later. I have mentioned the control wheel, which on many pioneer machines was turned, in its logical sense, either to warp the wings or to move the ailerons, but for crispness of control this was soon succeeded by the single control column, or joystick, used on nearly all machines for many years; eventually the wheel returned to use, firstly on the heavier aircraft and gradually, in the form of the yoke, it crept back into the lighter types and today there are many more machines with half-wheels than with sticks. Also the 1907 and 1909 Bleriots had tailwheels, but most later machines had skids at the rear; tail wheels (which were really practicable only when brakes were fitted) were not in full use again until well into the thirties.

The popular monoplane principle developed not only in performance and all-round capability, but noticeably in appearance. The Bleriot XI's rear fuselage structure was uncovered and fully exposed for all to see, while the Deperdussin, little over a year younger, was fully dressed. Both had their tiny engines mounted externally on the fronts of the fuselages, but by 1911 Robert Blackburn's Mercury monoplane had a neat cowling covering the top half of its rotary radial engine. The Bleriot and Blackburn machines make interesting comparisons on a feature-by-feature basis, on progress generally and especially on cleanness of design.

Not all designers favoured the monoplane; biplanes and triplanes played leading parts in the progressive development of the aeroplane and examples of both are displayed at Old Warden. The 1910 Bristol Boxkite (exhibited in reproduction form) and developed from the famous Henry Farman, sported many unusual features, including a controllable foreplane, a biplane tail, three rudders, a four-wheel undercarriage, a pusher propeller, ailerons and a control stick. By contrast, A.V. Roe's Triplane of the same year, although again using four mainwheels, had the more customary warping wings and (apart from the third wing) a generally more convential layout.

Boxkites and even Bleriots had limited roles in the military field, but most machines produced before 1912 were intended and used mainly to pioneer the principles and performance of controlled flight. Air races and long distance contests, with significant awards for the winners, encouraged those with the urge to fly — and those with the foresight to sell flying, in the form of aeroplanes or lessons, or both — to compete to make powered aircraft as practicable as possible. That they were developed more rapidly than anyone could have anticipated was brought-about largely by the outside influence of war, but let us stop at this point to consider these earliest pioneering efforts and the flying machines that have survived as evidence. Where possible these are exhibited alongside each other and although they include some of the oldest aeroplanes in the world that fly still today, a human touch is added to the scene when we realise that all the subsequent development, to Concorde and space flight, has occurred within the lifespan of a normal person. This progress is displayed in the Collection in a special educational section called 'The Early Days of Flight'.

Details of the aeroplanes that represent the first few years of controlled flight appear on the pages that follow.

(The aeroplanes in this section are exhibited in No. 1 Hangar, which is the building nearest to the entrance gate.)

1909: BLERIOT TYPE XI   Acquired: 1935

Span: 29ft. 0ins.
Empty weight: 484 lbs.
Power: 25 hp Anzani 3-cylinder fan.

Louis Bleriot just managed to get into the air in 1907, in his tandem-wing machine 'Libellule'. In the same year he produced his more conventional Bleriot No. VII which was the first-ever monoplane with a tractor engine, enclosed fuselage, rear mounted tail unit, and two-wheel main undercarriage, with a tail wheel; shortly after came his No. VIII which, surprisingly, had ailerons. The Bleriot XI, however, reverted to wing-warping for lateral control and it was the first of his designs to be wholly successful; in this he proved the possibility of cross-country flying on 13th July 1909 by covering 25 miles from Etampes to Orleans at a maximum height of about 75 ft. This achievement opened his mind to the practicability of a Channel crossing, which had been unsuccessfully attemped by an Antoinette monoplane only six days after Bleriot's first cross-country.

Soon after 0430 on Sunday 25th July 1909, Louis Bleriot took off from the French coast and 40 minutes later he crash-landed in a field near Dover Castle, to become the first person to cross the English Channel in an aeroplane. The early start was necessary for several reasons: calm conditions were needed to ensure full controllability of the machine and a low temperature was required to provide a cool charge for the small engine. The Anzani produced barely enough power for long sustained flight and many say that a brief rain shower cooled it sufficiently to help to keep it running, although a recent check on several contemporary daily newspapers reveals no trace of this. If the

shower story is true is it possible that, unwittingly, Bleriot was a pioneer in gaining benefits from water injection?

Following this success, Bleriot's monoplanes sold well and many flying schools adopted them as standard trainers. They were used in races and competitions and even in military roles. A Bleriot with the more powerful 50 hp Gnome rotary engine was used for the first aerial post from Hendon to Windsor in September 1911.

The Exhibit: BAPC 3. Basically similar to the machine used for the Channel crossing, this machine (constructor's No. 14) was one of the original aircraft on the Bleriot School at Hendon in 1910. It crashed in 1912, was stored under Blackfriars railway bridge and acquired by A.E. Grimmer who rebuilt and flew it. Richard Shuttleworth obtained it in 1935 and flew it in R.Ae.S. garden parties in 1937, 8 & 9. It suffered a minor accident in 1977, but has been repaired and is flying again. It is restricted to straight hops across the aerodrome.

1910: DEPERDUSSIN   Acquired 1935

Span: 28ft. 9ins.
Empty Weight: 500 lbs.
Power: 35 hp Anzani Y - type

During the short period between the birth of the Bleriot XI and the dimensionally similar Deperdussin, the Anzani engine had been developed from an out-of-balance fan layout to a more practicable Y shape that led to the later introduction of the popular and successful radial. The smoother running that this produced, together with a 30% increase in output, the sleeker design of the aeroplane and a totally covered fuselage, combined to produce a performance, which though hardly startling, made sustained flight a more regular reality.

The makers produced these machines in quantity to equip flying schools in Britain and on the Continent, with a selling price for the 'Popular' model set at £460. Although the Bleriot's earlier Channel crossing had made international history, the Deperdussin proved its practicability not by virtual wave or hedge-hopping, but by sustained cross-country flights at safer altitudes; in 1911 one came third in the Daily Mail Circuit of

Britain contest, flying from Hendon to Edinburgh, across to Glasgow and then via Carlisle, Manchester, Bristol, Exeter, Salisbury and Brighton to the famous historic flying ground at Brooklands.

Throughout the history of aviation, successful airframe designs have been developed by fitting more powerful engines. The 'Dep' was no exception and, as with the Bleriot, the 50 hp Gnome rotary was a logical and successful choice. Later, two and three-seater versions were produced each using Gnomes of higher power. In various forms and with engines of up to 100 hp, Deperdussins achieved many successful flights and established a share of records. A developed racing version achieved 124 mph in 1913, compared with the maximum of 55 mph credited to the basic machine; a seaplane version with a Gnome developing 160 hp won the first Schneider Trophy race at Monaco, achieving 127 mph. The pilot was Maurice Prevost.

The Exhibit: BAPC 4. A school or 'Popular' version, it is believed to be the 43rd to have been built, in 1910, and used at Hendon until offered for sale in damaged form in 1914. As with the Collection's Bleriot, it became the property of A.E. Grimmer who repaired and flew it from the polo ground near Bedford. When acquired by Richard Shuttleworth in 1935, it was in poor condition and it was renovated at Old Warden to fly again in 1937. Stored throughout World War II, it has flown several times in recent years and when weather conditions are ideal it is capable of completing a half circuit of the aerodrome, although normally it is restricted to 'straights'

1910: BRISTOL BOXKITE   Acquired 1966

Span: 34ft 6ins (upper mainplanes version military 46ft 6ins)
Empty Weight: 800 lbs (military 900 lbs)
Engines: various, including 50 hp and 70 hp Gnome rotary.
(This specimen has a modern 90 hp Lycoming)

In 1907 Henry Farman, often referred to as Henri Farman, but who was an Englishman living in France, started to modify a Voisin biplane to improve its performance and handling qualities. By 1909 he had designed his own machine, which he called Henry Farman III, and this proved to be one of the greatest aeroplanes of its time. Many people copied it and, in Britain, the result was the Bristol Boxkite.

The Boxkite was a striking sight; with elevators ahead of and behind the mainplanes, a biplane tail, three rudders and a pusher propeller, its prospects were based on refining and improving the Farman design, starting life with the bonus of a successful and well-proven type record behind it. Although essentially civil in origin, the Boxkite had clear military potential; in March 1911 four examples were ordered by the War Office at a time when many senior officers and politicians were opposed to the introduction of the aeroplane which, they insisted, could never replace the horse. A developed Service variant sported an additional 12 feet of span to the upper wing, to enable it to carry heavier loads.

Unlike many machines of the period, the Boxkite used ailerons for lateral control; but they were different from later ailerons, for they had no balance cables and hung 'limp' until the machine moved and the airflow lifted them into the flying attitude.

Boxkites were used in many parts of the world, including Australia and India; they were the first British aircraft to be ordered for export, with eight for the Imperial Russian Army. Although very successful, the type was cumbersome and had a relatively short life, with the last specimen flying in Australia late in 1915.

The Exhibit: BAPC 2. One of only two aircraft in the Collection that is not a genuine original historic machine, the Boxkite is a reproduction built by F.G. Miles Ltd at Shoreham for the film "Those Magnificent Men in their Flying Machines'. As no original Boxkite exists, the Bristol Aeroplane Co. Ltd acquired this specimen when the filming was finished and passed it to the Collection for preservation. In the air it is a most impressive sight, but it is flown only in conditions of almost complete calm.

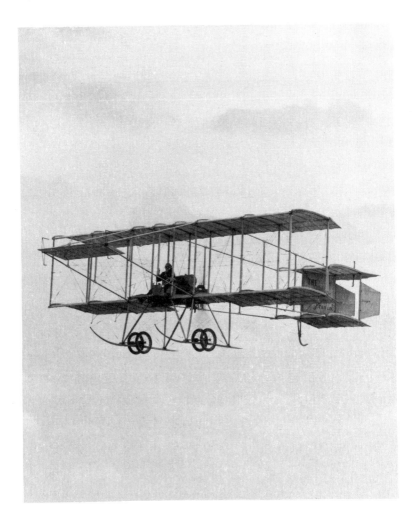

1910: AVRO TRIPLANE IV   Acquired 1966

Span: 32ft. (bottom wing 20ft.)
Empty weight: 650 lbs.
Power: 35 hp Green in-line (water cooled).
(This specimen has a 105 hp Cirrus Hermes II of 1927

A.V. Roe, who was one of Britain's most famous early pioneers, broke away from the usual monoplane or biplane layout and decided that a third set of wings would provide the lifting performance that he sought. He designed and built four such machines, which flew successfully, but which were used only for test and development. No version of the Avro Triplane was put into quantity production, but experience with these machines enabled him to design a highly successful biplane in the Avro 504; this, from 1913 onward and in a variety of versions, became the first really effective dual-control training aeroplane to be used on a large scale and the type remained in use into the thirties.

The triplane layout was based largely on a search for wings with a long span relative to the width (chord), resulting in what is known technically as a high aspect ratio. This has certain

aerodynamic advantages, stemming from the early discovery that most lift comes from the front portion, or just behind the leading edge of a wing, so the greater the span, the greater the lift that is produced. Another important advantage, however, is that the higher this ratio, the less the induced drag that is generated, therefore producing a better performance for a given power output. The Triplane IV had a remarkable aspect (span-to-chord) ratio of more than nine to one; clearly it proved its worth, for both the Avro 504 and the later Avro Tutor had wings that were long in relation to their width.

The Triplane had a control wheel, which, when turned, twisted the shape of the outer sections of the two upper sets of wings, to provide lateral control through wing warping. The shorter bottom wing, mounted below and clear of the fuselage so that lift could be generated throughout its span, was not connected to the control system.

The name Avro, derived from A.V. Roe, lived in the lead of famous British aeroplanes through both world wars and beyond; the Anson and the Lancaster are household names, while the Vulcan which remains in service with the Royal Air Force into the late eighties, also is of Avro origin.

The Exhibit: BAPC 1. With the Boxkite this shares the claim to be a relatively recently-built machine, for this, too, was constructed for the film 'Those Magnificent Men in their Flying Machines', by the Hampshire Aeroplane Club at Eastleigh, Southampton. Although the original Roe Triplane is in the Science Museum, this reproduction was of considerable technical interest and an impressive flyer, so the Trustees decided that it should be acquired to add to the Collection.

1912: BLACKBURN   Acquired 1938

Span: 35ft. 8ins.
Empty Weight: 550 lbs.
Power: 50 hp Gnome rotary.

Robert Blackburn was one of Britain's pioneers in designing and building aeroplanes. The first of his machines to fly successfully did so from the sands at Filey in 1910 and several developments followed over the next two years. The basic type became known as the Mercury and the machine in the Collection is the seventh and one of the last of that line, completed in 1912. By this time the design had improved into one of clean overall layout, with all surfaces fully covered and even a cowling round the top half of the engine, but still using wing-warping for lateral control.

The name of Blackburn survived until well after World War II when it became absorbed into Hawker-Siddeley Aviation. The Baffin, Shark, Skua, Roc and Botha are among the types remembered from that era, while among the last to emerge with the Blackburn prefix were the huge Beverley heavy transport for the RAF and the Buccaneer low-level strike aircraft. In addition to aeroplanes, the company produced numerous aero engines including the Cirrus Major, the Cirrus Minor and the Bombardier. Also the firm ran two reserve flying schools for the Royal Air Force and these were the only units to be equipped with the Blackburn B2 side-by-side biplane trainer; a flying specimen of this 1932 product is retained today at its birthplace of Brough in East Yorkshire.

The Exhibit: BAPC 5. Built to the order of Cyril Foggin who learned to fly at the Blackburn School at Hendon; later acquired by Francis Glew, but stored in 1914 and not discovered until 1937, largely hidden in a haystack. Then obtained by Richard Shuttleworth, who started to restore it, but work was not completed until 1949. In calm conditions it flies a slow, majestic circuit and makes its mark as the oldest genuine original British aeroplane still to fly anywhere in the world.

Chapter 3
The Pressure of War

The first flying machines were just that; they had no roles to perform other than the essential achievement of successful flight. This is logical in the early evolution process, but clearly there would be many functions for which an aeroplane would be tasked. War was one. Although at the outbreak of the Great War in 1914 military aeronautical activity was both minimal and disorganised, with considerable opposition from the diehards who predicted that the aeroplane could be no match for the horse, very little time passed between the light and relatively flimsy pre-war structures and the strong, workhorse machines of the mid-teens. Perhaps the production Blackburn monoplane of 1912 and the appearance of the Bristol Fighter only four years later can bring home this point most effectively.

Just as the aeroplanes of the Air Batallion of the Royal Engineers (which merged in 1912 into the Royal Flying Corps) and the first equipment of the Royal Naval Air Service could not be described as machines with obvious fighting potential, the available equipment with which to wage war in the air was equally sparse. Although wireless communication was tried experimentally in the earliest days, suitable sets were not regularly available and other methods were used for passing information; message streamers, for example, were dropped for passing details of the enemy's whereabouts. On the fighting front, revolvers or rifles were used from cockpits, and these led to very personal duels between individual opponents; some bombs, including the 20lb Hale, existed from the outset and grenades were dropped, but even darts — or flechettes as they were called — were released from cockpits. For a short time these were dropped in large numbers onto troop concentrations in the hope that quantity would produce devastating results, but there is little evidence that they were particularly effective.

Specimens of these early tools of war are displayed in the Collection with uniforms, helmets, flight instruments (note the size of the airspeed indicator used in the Handley Page 0/400 of 1917) and documents relating to the whole 1914-18 era. But perhaps one of the most significant achievements of the mid-war period was the ability to fire a fixed forward-facing machine gun through the arc of a revolving propeller. This was achieved by synchronising gears, well-known examples of which were the Constantinesco (hydraulic) and Sopwith-Kauper (mechanical) interruptor gears; these devices had a major impact on the ability of the aeroplane to engage in serious combat; the gun could be mounted on top of the fuselage, within reach of the pilot, who not only aimed it (and his aeroplane) at the target, but could deal with technical management of the gun itself. A diagram is on display to show the way in which the hydraulic interruptor gear worked.

The aeroplane and its equipment developed together; the flexible monoplane structure with its need for bracing from above and below gave way to a biplane layout that offered several advantages. Admittedly an extra wing generated more drag (wind resistance) but this was relatively uncritical at the low speed of the time; more important was the biplane's additional lift, which helped in carrying the heavier loads associated with a military operation. However, the biplane's main advantage was its structural rigidity, for gone were the pylons, to be replaced by streamline inter-plane struts near the tips and strong attachments or mountings to the fuselage at the inboard ends of the wings. The biplane, too, could have a smaller span for a given weight-lifting ability, and this improved both the roll rate and overall manoeuvrability.

There were a few exceptions to the biplane trend, but the 1914-18 aeroplanes on view at Old Warden are representative of the general concept of the time. A remarkable commonality existed; most machines were single-engine tractor (i.e. propeller at the front) biplanes, with two main-wheels and tailskids and, for those accommodating two crew members, cockpits in tandem. Perhaps some of the greatest variations were in engine design; in the early part of the war, the rotary radial achieved both success and fame. On this, the crankshaft was fixed to the airframe structure and the crankcase and cylinders revolved round it. There was no carburettor as such; petrol was delivered through the hollow crankshaft and the air/fuel ratio was controlled by the pilot with two side-by-side levers to enable him to achieve the required fine adjustment; critical this was, too, for either a lean or a rich mixture would produce a power cut, so once the day's optimum setting (which varied with temperature, pressure, humidity and other factors) had been found by pre-take-off experiment, many pilots tended to leave this well alone. Then performance control was the work of the 'blip switch'; this was a button on the stick, which, when depressed, cut out the ignition, the power returning when the button was released.

Rotary engines had short working lives, many being cleared for only fifty hours between overhauls, but aeroplanes' operational lives, too, were usually clipped prematurely in battle or in accident, so this was not its most serious shortcoming. The disadvantage was that the large, heavy rotating mass produced strong gyroscopic effects, so that when turning in one direction the nose of the aircraft tended to fall and, in turning the other way, to rise. This made manoeuvring and accurate gun-sighting difficult and had restricting effects on the tactics of the time.

When running well, with all cylinders firing, the rotary was a remarkably smooth power source, and the reliability record was better than one might expect from an all-moving engine; but, although used in trainers for many more years, by 1917 its operational heyday had passed. The static engine had been developed to a remarkable performance level, with the Rolls-Royce Falcon producing 275 h.p. and heralding a design layout that held (and perhaps led) the field for thirty years. A liquid-cooled engine with 12 cylinders in a V layout, the Falcon's logical and progressively developed successors were the Kestrel, Merlin and Griffon, the last of these serving into the eighties with the Royal Air Force's remaining squadron of Shackletons. It is unlikely that any basic concept (except, perhaps, the wing!) has remained to the fore for such a large percentage of aviation's history to date.

Although the aeroplanes of the 1914-18 war live on at Old Warden, to be seen statically at close quarters on any day and occasionally in the air, we must not forget the people involved. The flying personnel, with descriptive showcases devoted to the achievements of such aces as Major James McCudden and Captain Albert Ball, V.C. (both of whom flew Royal Aircraft Factory SE5s that were similar to the example now on display) are key figures, but no aeroplane has been able to fly without the hard and skilled efforts of those whose work has remained unsung; not only the ground crews in the field, but also the hundreds of women who sewed the fabric that covered the greater part of all the aeroplanes of the time. Photographs of these, too, serve to remind us of the national effort behind the wartime aviation scene.

Many readers may be surprised at the scale of the flying operation in the first war. Allegedly more than 8,000 Avro 504s were built and, although accident rates were high with frequent write-offs, in November 1918 the Royal Air Force had 22,647 aeroplanes on active strength. Only a few of these have survived, but the representative types on show serve as rare reminders of one of the most hectic periods of aerial activity that the world has known.

(Hangar No. 2 is devoted to aircraft of World War I, but see also Hangar No. 4)

1915 AVRO 504K   Acquired 1958

Span: 36ft. 0ins.
Empty weight: 1231 lbs.
Power: 110 hp le Rhone rotary
(but several others used)

Following A.V. Roe's experiments with a triplane formula, (see page 31) he continued his policy of using wings with high aspect ratio, but in bi-plane form. The result emerged as the Avro

504, which from its 1913 debut had an unusually long and successful career, at least four specimens surviving for impressment into military Service at the start of World War II.

The 504 entered the Royal Flying Corps as a fighting aeroplane and although used largely for observation purposes, bringing back information on enemy troop movements (against a strong resentment from the army commanders who saw no use for aircraft) the type was one of the first to be adapted for the bombing role; in November 1914 four Avro 504s made history by carrying out the first pre-planned bombing attack, with the Zeppelin works at Friedrichshafen as their target. It was in the training field, though, that the Avro 504 made its mark. Powered by the 100 hp Gnome Monosoupape, the 504J was the standard equipment of the School of Special Flying at Gosport in Hampshire where the Commanding Officer, Major R. Smith-Barry, evolved the first organised pilot training system that formed the foundations of the R.A.F.'s later syllabus. Also it was the type on which King George VI learnt to fly. The K version, usually powered by the 100 hp le Rhone, but capable of taking a variety of rotary engines including the 130 hp Clerget and even the 150 hp Bentley BR-1, remained in R.A.F. service until replaced in the late twenties by the Lynx-engined 504N.

Many surplus Ks were used after World War I by civil operators, mainly to provide joy-rides; individual modifications extended some of these into three or even four-seaters.

The Exhibit: Built in 1918 as a K(H5199), converted in R.A.F. service to a 504N and later civilianised as G-ADEV. Winner of the Devon Air Race in 1937 at 103 mph. Impressed into military service in 1940 as BK892 for glider towing experiments. Subsequently re-converted to original K standard by Avro apprentices for the Collection. The displayed serial E3404 is spurious, but was used initially as the true identity was not known at the time of conversion.

1916 SOPWITH PUP   Acquired 1937

Span: 26ft. 6ins.
Empty weight: 787 lbs.
Power: 80 hp le Rhone rotary

The Sopwith Pup was ordered early in 1916 for the Royal Naval Air Service and the type was used for trials of landing on the deck of a ship under way at sea, the results of which led to the development of the operational aircraft carrier. Later forming the equipment of several squadrons of the Royal Flying Corps, the Pup served with distinction on the Western Front from December 1916 onward.

Although relatively low-powered, the Pup was manoeuvrable. Its light weight helped to provide a good rate of climb and an ability to hold its height in combat; successful encounters at 15,000 feet or more were not unknown. Standard armament was a single Vickers gun mounted in front of the pilot on top of the fuselage, synchronised to fire through the arc of the propeller by Sopwith-Kauper mechanical interrupter gear.

The operational life of the Pup was quite short by comparison with that of its higher-powered stablemate the Camel, but even the latter remained in squadron service for only a short time after the end of the war, when the Snipe replaced it. The Sopwith Aviation Company, though, endeavoured to put the last Pups on the production line into civilian use by converting them to two-seaters and using the appropriate peacetime name Dove. Drawings of the Pup have remained available from British Aerospace at Kingston-upon-Thames as today's successors to the Sopwith Company; as a result, several modern reproductions of the Pup have been built.

The Exhibit: Constructor's No. W/O 3004/14. The last of ten Pups converted on the 1918 production line to two-seat civil Doves. Registered G-EBKY. Owned by C.H. Low-Wylde and based at West Malling; acquired by Richard Shuttleworth in 1936 and re-converted at Old Warden to original Pup standard. Not originally allocated a Service serial, so spuriously marked N5180, which was the Pup prototype.

1917 BRISTOL F.2b   Acquired 1952

Span: 39ft. 3ins.
Empty Weight: 1934 lbs.
Power: 275 hp Rolls-Royce Falcon III V-12

The British and Colonial Aeroplane Company designed a number of aeroplanes after the Boxkite of 1910 (see page 28) so by 1916 considerable experience was available for the development of the Bristol Fighter. The type entered service with the Royal Flying Corps on the Western front in March 1917. A large, rugged two-seater, the Bristol F.2b became well-respected by its opponents and earned the reputation of being the most effective fighting aeroplane of the first world war.

Various engines were used including the Hispano-Suiza, Siddeley Puma, Wolseley Viper and Sunbeam Arab, but the most successful was the Rolls-Royce Falcon liquid-cooled 12-cylinder Vee. Standard armanent was a fixed Vickers gun firing forward through the propeller arc with a Constantinesco sychronising gear and one (sometimes two) Lewis gun(s) mounted on a Scarff ring and controlled by the rearward-facing observer. After initial difficulties, this back-to-back teamwork proved very effective.

Although deservedly famous for its wartime success, the F.2b continued in production until 1926 and earned its reputation over a long period in service. Peacetime duties at home were largely on army co-operation work, while squadrons served overseas in such diverse areas as Germany, Turkey, Iran and India. The final role was a dual-control trainer with Oxford and Cambridge University Air Squadrons, from which the type was retired in 1932.

The Exhibit: D 8096. Built in 1918. No wartime operational service, but with No. 208 Squadron in Turkey in 1923. Acquired in 1936 by Captain C.P.B. Ogilvie, who stored it at Primrose Garages, Watford, with the aim of refurbishing to flying condition. Civil registration G-AEPH allotted but not used. Restored by the Bristol Aeroplane Company and first flown in Shuttleworth ownership in February 1952. After 28 years with the Collection, underwent extensive engine and airframe refurbishing in Old Warden workshops in 1980-82.

1917 ROYAL AIRCRAFT FACTORY S.E.5a   Acquired 1957

Span: 26 ft. 9 ins.
Empty weight: 1530 lbs.
Power: 200 hp Wolseley Viper V-8

The Royal Aircraft Factory at Farnborough (predecessor of today's Royal Aircraft Establishment) designed and built the S.E.5 single-seat scout around the availability of the French 150 hp Hispano Suiza engine. The type went into active service in France in April 1917. Modifications to the airframe and development of the geared engine to produce 200 hp resulted in the S.E.5a, which became one of the most successful fighters of the war. An alternative power source was the 200 hp Wolseley Viper, which was less complicated as it was a direct-drive engine.

Armed with two forward-firing machine guns, with a Vickers on top of the fuselage (using synchronising gear to avoid bullets hitting the propeller) and a Lewis mounted on top of the wing centre section and operated by a Bowden cable running to the cockpit, the S.E.5 and S.E.5a were the mounts of many of the aces of the time; among these were Major J. McCudden and Captain Albert Ball, V.C.

43

At the end of the war, 16 squadrons of the Royal Air Force were equipped with the S.E.5a, but although its subsequent front-line military career lasted only a year or so, the type started a fresh civilian life; it proved popular as a sporting machine and competed in many air races (including the once-only Oxford and Cambridge Air Race of 1921 in which six participated), but its most notable peacetime achievement was in sky-writing. Major J.C. Savage's machines were in great demand for aerial advertising throughout Britain, while eleven S.E.5a's were used in the United States of America for similar work. The last airworthy S.E.5a in Britain made its final flight in 1937.

The Exhibit: Used in 1924 by Major Savage as G-EBIA. Found in 1955 hanging from the roof of the Armstrong-Whitworth flight shed at Whitley and subsequently restored for the Collection by staff and apprentices at R.A.E. Farnborough, where it first flew in again August 1959. Following problems with the Hispano-Suiza, the engine was changed in 1975 to a Wolseley Viper. Now flying in military markings with Service serial F904. Sometimes away at R.A.E.

1917 LUFT-VERKEHRS-GESELLSCHAFT LVG CVI

Acquired 1966

Span: 42ft. 5ins. (upper wings)
Empty weight: 2090 lbs.
Power 230 hp Benz upright in-line

The LVG CIV was the first aeroplane to make a daylight raid on London — in November 1916. A development, the CV, entered large scale service with the Imperial German Air Force and was used for observation and light bombing duties. The ultimate variant, the CVI, differed in having a deepened fuselage, reduced wing gap and a raised position for the observer-gunner to improve his field of view. Armament was a single fixed Spandau gun offset to the starboard side of the cockpit, firing forward through the propeller and one movable Parabellum gun operated from the rear cockpit.

The LVG CVI was a strong and steady observation platform, but was large, heavy and relatively cumbersome on the handling side. Although it achieved considerable success in its intended role, lack of manoeuvrability made it a favourite target for British fighter pilots.

The Benz engine was a rugged, slow-revving unit with six cylinders in line and a vertical exhaust stack giving the impression of a steam engine. This layout, while strange to British eyes, was used by the Germans on several other types.

Several CVIs were taken over at the end of the war and the type was extensively flight-tested for evaluation purposes in comparision with British types such as the Bristol Fighter.

The Exhibit: 7198/18 (the last figure indicating the year of manufacture). Believed to have been assembled from two or three machines captured in 1918; subsequently flown by the R.A.F. at Martlesham Heath. Stored for many years by the Air Ministry Air Historical Branch and loaned for a time to the Science Museum, but not exhibited; appeared in mock combat with a Sopwith Triplane, a Bristol Fighter and SE5a at the 1937 Hendon Air Pageant. Passed to the Collection on long loan in 1966 and restored to flying condition at Old Warden, jointly by the Collection's engineering staff and specialist members of the Shuttleworth Veteran Aeroplane Society.

Chapter 4
Private Flying between the Wars

At the end of World War 1 many hundreds of surplus military aeroplanes became available for civil use and these were sold at prices that were tiny fractions of their original costs. Many were handled by the Aircraft Disposal Company and among the types to find ready buyers were the Avro 504 and SE 5a, both of which have been described in the previous chapter. On a smaller scale, attempts were made by the manufacturers to convert machines on their existing production lines into civilian material; the Sopwith Aviation Company's two-seat Dove (as an on-the-line modification from the military single-seat Pup) was one example, but for reasons of expense most sales were centred on the surplus machines that had seen varying amounts of military service.

This ready supply of serviceable aeroplanes, some of which were nearly new, virtually eliminated any immediate post-war demand for new conventional light civil aeroplanes, so the makers turned their minds to economy in a manner that would be appropriate in today's approaching energy crisis. The aim was to obtain maximum performance from minimum power, resulting in quite fantastic returns of miles flown for each gallon used. In 1923 the English Electric Wren, with its diminutive two-cylinder ABC engine of only 398 cc, competed with success at the Daily Mail Light Aeroplane Contest at Lympne in Kent by covering 87.5 miles on one gallon.

In the same year Geoffrey de Havilland came forward with the little DH53, a single-seater powered by a range of small engines including the 750 cc Douglas, 698 cc Blackburne Tomtit and the Bristol Cherub. Although it flew successfully, experience proved it to be too light and too small for really practical use; the DH 51, by contrast, was a moderate-size biplane that could seat two - three people, but this, too, failed to fill a need in the market. Not to be beaten, the de Havilland name excelled itself when the first DH 60 Moth appeared. In effect this was a mid-way design between the extremes of the DH 51 and 53, but if ever a compromise could be successful, the Moth proved the point.

Perhaps the Moth is the most significant of the production light aeroplanes of the period shortly after World War 1. With the supply of former military machines exhausted and with light aeroplane clubs being formed in many parts of Britain, by 1925 a new market had materialised. The Moth was ideal; simple, rugged, reliable and economical, yet large and powerful enough for serious flights to be carried out effectively, it filled the bill for training, touring, competitions and record-breaking.

Private and sporting flying would have grown in popularity far less rapidly if the DH 60 had been missing from the inventory. From the original design, the Moth breed later extended into a range of machines to suit all tastes, contributing in no small way to Britain's reputation for producing the world's most successful light aircraft. Other manufacturers followed in attempts to fill the new demand, but none quite managed to equal the magic of the Moths.

The two-seat open biplane, in most cases with cockpits in tandem, was the norm of the day, but some designers spread their thoughts in many directions to produce machines ranging from single-seat ultra-lights, suitable for amateur construction, to refined cabin monoplanes for those seeking comfort, speed and range. The contrasting result can be seen at Old Warden today in the Flying Flea and the Percival Gull-Six. The first, of French origin, with a top speed of about 60 mph behind (among others) a Scott motorcycle engine of 16 hp was intended to be suitable for the absolute beginner who could build it and then teach himself to fly it; the second offered 200 hp, a top speed of about 175 mph and a cabin for three. Both are described separately on their own pages later in the book, but by mentioning them together we can appreciate the diversity of ideas and needs that were spreading into the realm of the light aeroplane; similar extremes exist today although, alas, in recent years there have been no British machines to maintain the national reputation built-up in the twenties and thirties. Certainly from 1981 two types of training/touring monoplane are in limited production, but they have entered the sales arena at a difficult time to make any penetration into a market that has been held by America for nearly three decades.

The Collection is fortunate to hold a very broad range of civil types of the period between the wars, when the use and development of the true light aeroplane reached its climax. One hangar, opened in 1982, houses an exclusive range of aircraft of de Havilland origin, while another covers the field of products of the other manufacturers of the time. No one should deny the practical value of the designs of the seventies and eighties, for some very usable aircraft are available on the world market, but values have changed. Today the main aims are to produce aircraft that are geared to quantity production, easy to fly and which can accommodate advanced avionics (radio equipment) to simplify the task of navigating en route and letting down to aerodromes in bad weather. From a workaday angle, these intentions are wholly logical and beneficial, but by eliminating the need for accurate handling and reducing the requirement for such a built-in consciousness of wind and weather, the modern designer has deprived pilots of many of the skills and pleasures that have been associated with pure flying for its own sake.

A modern aeroplane on a tricycle undercarriage is easy to steer on the ground and the tendency to weathervane into wind is noticeable only in the roughest conditions, while the light aeroplane pilot in a biplane with a brakeless tail-skid undercarriage needs to work constantly with throttle, rudder and sometimes aileron to attain and maintain the desired headings. An out-of-wind take-off in the earlier machine calls for comparable skills; once in the air balanced flight requires co-ordinated use of hands and feet with accurate use of the rudder to match the control in roll; even more, a landing on all three points results only from a well-adjusted approach at the right speed, with accurate judgment of the height and rate of hold-off; keeping straight at the end of a landing run in certain conditions can demand rapid response with rudder before a slight swing develops into something worse.

More about flying a typical biplane of the period between the wars appears in a later chapter and detailed handling descriptions of many of the historic aeroplanes are contained in a companion volume to this book (From Bleriot to Spitfire: flying the historic aeroplanes of the Shuttleworth Collection), but the marked changes in flight characteristics that have occurred in the recent post-war years have made the modern light aeroplane into something that is so fundamentally different from its predecessor of forty or so years ago. That in itself enhances the value of the range of earlier types housed in the Collection and adds to the importance of keeping these machines in flying condition.

In the pages that follow, you will find descritions of the many light civil aeroplanes of the twenties and thirties that comprise the private and sporting flying section of the Collection. The list is long, for there is no obvious break point right up to the end of civil aircraft production on the outbreak of war in 1939. In some cases aircraft have claims to fame in both civil and Service roles. Those that fall specifically within this band and which could be included in the present chapter are the de Havilland DH 89A (Rapide in civil form or Dominie in service guise) but the example on display is in military markings and therefore finds a place in chapter 5; also on the fringe are the DH 82A Tiger Moth and Miles M 14a Magister (Hawk Trainer), but as their military numbers were the greater, they, too, have been placed in sequence in the later chapter. (The aeroplanes described in this section are exhibited in No. 3 and No. 7 hangars — the latter housing aircraft of de Havilland origin).

1923 ENGLISH ELECTRIC WREN   Acquired 1957

Span: 37ft. 0ins.
Empty weight: 232 lbs.
Power: 398 cc A.B.C. horizontal twin.

Although known mainly for its success in the Light Aeroplane Trials at Lympne, Kent, in 1923, the Wren flew two years before this when the first machine was built to Air Ministry order and serialled J6973. The idea was to produce an ultra-light training aeroplane of very low structure weight and capable of operating on very low power. Such a search for the ultimate in economy might seem more appropriate today, when we are faced with growing energy supply problems, but clearly cost was a hazard in the years shortly after the Great War.

The Wren's success at Lympne earned the type a lasting reputation, for in the trial one of the two contest machines flew 87.5 miles on one gallon of fuel, an achievement that it shared with the little ANEC monoplane, a dismantled specimen of which exists in the Collection. Clearly an aeroplane with such a small engine as that in the Wren would require all available power in order to achieve a sustained and positive climb, and there is no record of a Wren managing to fly higher than about

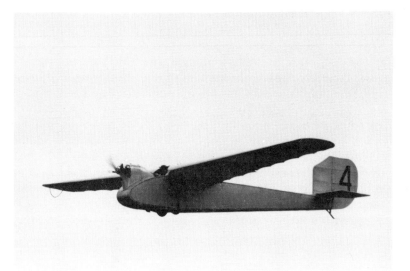

1200 feet. Overall performance was such that flights were practical only in conditions of favourable wind and weather, so, along with other underpowered designs of the twenties, the Wren failed to attract a production order. Three Wrens were built, but mild confusion was caused by the constructor's numbers, which not only included a No. 4, but Nos. 3 and 4 flew with reversed identities, the first ture civil registration not being allocated until 1926, when No. 4, flying as No. 3, became G-EBNV!

The Exhibit: Basically No. 4 (c/n3) which was one of the Lympne machines, presented to the Collection by R.H. Grant of Dumfries; rebuilt by the English Electric Company by including many components from No. 3 (c/n 4) supplied by the Science Museum. Flown at Warton in January 1957 and handed-over at the Royal Aeronautical Society's Garden Party later that year. Extensively refurbished again at Warton in 1980 and returned to the Shuttleworth flying fleet early in 1981.

1923 DH 53 HUMMING BIRD   Acquired 1954

Span: 30ft. 1in.
Empty weight: 326 lbs.
Power: 34 hp A.B.C. Scorpion horizontal twin (originally 750 cc Douglas)

The DH 53 was the first light aeroplane produced by the de Havilland Aircraft Company; two specimens were built in time for the famous Daily Mail light aeroplane trials at Lympne in 1923, at which the test pilot Hubert Broad impressed everyone present by performing loops and rolls on such a low-powered machine. This original 750 cc Douglas motorcycle engine, however, proved troublesome and all twelve production aircraft were fitted with 698 cc Blackburne Tomtit engines that developed 26 hp. Other engines used were the Bristol Cherub and A.B.C. Scorpion, both of which were horizontally-opposed two-cylinder units.

The DH 53 is thought of as a civil aeroplane and therefore appears in this section, but after the two Lympne aircraft the eight machines built for British use started their careers with the Royal Air Force, initially for evaluation as trainers but

subsequently used on communications duties. Two were specially equipped for hooking trials with the airship R-33 and on 4th December 1925 the first release and re-engagement were successfully carried out with J 7325. Other DH 53s went abroad direct to civil customers; three to Australia, one to Czechoslovakia and the final example to Russia.

All eight RAF machines survived to be released in 1927, most to be put through the Royal Aircraft Establishment Aero Club at Farnborough for their Certificates of Airworthiness. Although too light and low-powered for popularity, with no production order for the British civil market, the ex-Service specimens flew for several years, the last, G-EBXN, passing through seven owners before being retired in 1938 and burned two years later.

The Exhibit: G-EBHX: One of the two original Lympne contestants. Found without engine in a shed near Deal in Kent by Squadron Leader L.A. Jackson, then the Collection's manager. Restored by the DH Technical School at Hatfield and fitted with A.B.C. Scorpion, to fly on 4th August 1960. Engine problems have prevented this diminutive machine from being a popular performer among the Shuttleworth pilots or engineers.

1924 DH 51   Acquired 1972;
Span: 37ft. 0ins.
Empty weight: 1342 lbs.
Power: 120 hp Airdisco 8-cylinder upright V.
(originally 90 hp RAF 1a)

To present a guide in chronological order the author faces several problems. Surely the DH 51 should appear before the DH 53? In practice the 51 flew ten months later than the 53 and this seems to be sufficient justification for the present arrangement.

Although the precise reason for the 51's late appearance is difficult to determine, the most likely cause was the lack of a suitable engine. War surplus 90 hp Royal Aircraft Factory RAF 1a's were available and, although heavy and with only single ignition, one was fitted to the first machine of the type, G-EBIM, which flew in July 1924. However, the French Renault engine was being developed for civil use and, by fitting aluminium cylinder heads and other modifications, its output was increased from 80 to 120 hp to become the Airdisco. Remotored, 'IM flew again and obtained a C of A three months later.

The DH 51 was designed to accommodate two people and luggage, or three people, with a sliding top fuselage fairing to adjust the layout. Although well-liked and very docile, it proved rather large for the average owner's needs (which meant that hangarage was expensive) and only three were built. The first went to Australia and was converted to a seaplane, but capsized in Sydney harbour in 1931. The second was scrapped in 1933 and the third G-EBIR/VP-KAA became the first aircraft to be registered in Kenya, where it had an active existence lasting nearly 40 years.

The Exhibit: G-EBIR (VP-KAA). The third and last built. Airfreighted from Nairobi to Hatfield in 1965 and restored by Hawker-Siddeley Aviation (now a part of British Aerospace) at Hawarden, Chester. Flown to Old Warden in 1972 to be placed in the permanent care of the Collection, where it operates as the only specimen of the oldest design of de Havilland origin to fly anywhere in the world. It is a key exhibit in the new de Havilland Flying Centre.

1928 DH 60X MOTH   Acquired 1932

Span: 30ft. 0ins.
Empty weight: 955 lbs.
Power: 105 hp Hermes II 4-cylinder up-right in-line (originally 65 hp Cirrus 1)

The DH 60 Moth must be considered as one of the most successful light aeroplanes of all time. Following the inadequacies of the diminutive DH 53 and the rather overweight DH 51, the Moth proved itself a winner from its first flight in February 1925. Apart from the rightness of the airframe design, the newly-available Cirrus engine provided both the required power output and the essential economy to go with it. This unit was developed by virtually cutting the 8 cylinder Airdisco (see DH 51) in half, resulting in a 4 cylinder in-line that developed 60 hp for a weight of 290 lbs.

The light aeroplane movement owes much of its growth to the introduction of the DH 60 and officialdom must have been less hidebound than it is today; by mid-1925 Sir Samuel Hoare, then Secretary of State for Air, became interested in the possibilities and the Air Ministry (in those days responsible for civil as well as

military aviation) subsidised five flying clubs to be equipped with Moths: The Lancashire, London, Newcastle, Midland and Yorkshire.

Only three months after the first flight, Alan Cobham flew the prototype 1000 miles from Croydon to Zurich and back in a day and, by 1926, considerably more than half the aeroplanes attending flying meetings were Moths. Naturally the design was developed; an additional 25 hp was produced by the Cirrus II, with which many production machines were fitted. The Armstrong-Siddeley Genet 5-cylinder radial engine was used by the RAF Central Flying School in six Moths that performed formation aerobatics at the 1927 Hendon display. In the next year, most production machines used the 90 hp Cirrus III, but a more notable improvement was the redesigned undercarriage of the spilt rather than straight-axle type, resulting in the designation DH 60X. This gave a smoother ride and was much more forgiving of misjudged landings!

A description of the slightly later DH 60G Gipsy Moth follows.

The Exhibit: G-EBWD. Built in 1928 and bought by Richard Shuttleworth at Brooklands in 1932, as his first aeroplane. Remotored from Cirrus II to Hermes in 1933. After more than 50 years ʼWD has lived at one aerodrome (Old Warden) for longer than any flying aeroplane in aviation history.

1928 DH 60G MOTH   Acquired 1977

Span: 30ft. 0ins.
Empty weight: 920 lbs.
Power: 100 hp Gipsy I 4-cylinder upright in-line (some with 120 hp Gipsy II)

By early 1928 the famous Gipsy engine had been envolved by the de Havilland company and not surprisingly the first production units were earmarked for Moths. So the DH 60G Gipsy Moth was born as a logical successor to the already world-winning Cirrus variant.

One aim for headline hitting was to have the new machine ready for the 1928 King's Cup Air Race; this target was fulfilled, for 14 Moths were entered and three of these were Gipsy powered. One, G-EBYZ, became the winner after averaging a remarkable 105 mph round Britain. This was followed by many proving and publicity exercises: Captain Geoffrey de Havilland flew one to a record 21,000 ft and Hubert Broad remained airborne in another for 24 hours, but perhaps the most valuable achievement was an engine reliability trial, in which a production Gipsy I was sealed for 600 hours and required an expenditure on replacement parts of only £7.2.11 afterwards.

Gipsy Moths were exported in quantity and licence production was carried out in France, Australia and in the United States, while British-built machines held their heads high. Amy Johnson flew the famous 'Jason', G-AAAH (on display in the Science Museum) from Croydon to Darwin to become the first woman to fly from England to Australia. Francis Chichester achieved navigational fame when the found the diminutive Norfolk and Lord Howe islands in his float-fitted G-AAKK. John Grierson flew G-AAJP (a model of which is on show in the Collection) to Lahore, Baghdad, Moscow and Iceland. But we must not forget the hundreds of Gipsy Moths that provided popular and reliable mounts for the ordinary private and club pilots of the thirties.

The Exhibit: G-ABAG. Constructor's No. 1259. Built 1930 and registered to Bentley Motors Ltd. Four subsequent pre-war

owners; also loaned to the Stage and Screen Aero Club, during which time Ralph Richardson learnt to fly on it. Stored throughout 1939-45 war. Based at Perth from 1950 and subsequently owned alternately by brothers Douglas and Peter Hull. Sold to and crashed while in ownership of Strathtay Aero Club and returned to Hull brothers. After Douglas Hull's death, his widow presented it to the Shuttleworth Collection, where it made its first public demonstration on 28th August 1977, prior to a formal hand-over on 13th October.

1929 PARNALL ELF   Acquired 1951

Span: 31ft. 3ins.
Empty weight: 1020 lbs.
Power: 105 hp Hermes II 4-cylinder upright in-line.

The Parnall Elf made its public debut at Olympia in July 1929. This was the last in a line of aeroplanes designed by Harold Bolas, most of which were built by George Parnall and Co of Yate, near Bristol — a carpentry firm that had turned over to aircraft production during the Great War. Previous Parnall machines included the Pixie, which along with many other ultra-light designs had achieved success in the 1923 Lympne trials and one version of which flew successfully as both a biplane and a monoplane; and the Imp, of 1927, which although fitted initially with an Armstrong-Siddeley Genet was used later for flight-testing the first of the Pobjoy radial engines.

The Elf was a two-seater biplane designed for the private and club market, with folding wings for storage economy and intended to require only minimum maintenance. The customary array of flying and landing wires could be dispensed with, as the interplane struts were arranged to form a Warren girder structure. Fuel was pumped from the main fuselage supply to a small header tank in the top wing centre section, from which the engine was gravity fed.

Three were built: G-AAFH, G-AAIN and G-AAIO. 'FH and 'IO were destroyed in flying accidents in 1934. In that year the last machine to carry the Parnall name — the Hendy Heck — first flew; a low wing cabin monoplane, it went into small-scale production and a little-known 2-seat military trainer variant, the Heck 3, was remarkably similar in appearance to the better-known Miles Magister. Only one was constructed.

The Exhibit: G-AAIN. First flight June 1932. Owned by Lord Apsley at Badminton and stored throughout 1939-45 war. Based at Fairoaks and acquired by the Collection in non-flying condition in July 1951. Loaned for temporary static display to the Historic Aircraft Museum, Southend, in 1972. Subsequently fully restored at Old Warden by two former apprentices, to make its first public appearance in the air in August 1980.

1930 DH 80A PUSS MOTH   Loaned 1978

Span: 36ft. 9ins.
Empty weight: 1265 lbs.
Power: 130 hp Gipsy Major I inverted 4-cylinder in-line (at first 120 hp Gipsy III)

The open-cockpit Moths attracted many sporting pilots and their passengers, but some customers sought the comforts of the cabin, therefore removing the need to wear special flying clothing. To satisfy this demand, the de Havilland Aircraft Co. produced the unnamed DH 80 high-wing enclosed tandem 2-

seater. A Gipsy II engine, which had been designed to run upright (with the cylinders pointing upward) was modified to operate in the inverted attitude, which provides improved view for the pilot and a greater propeller ground clearance.

The DH 80 first flew in September 1929. Before production started, however, the original wooden fuselage structure was changed to one of welded steel tube, a door on the right side only was balanced by fitting one on each side and other refinements included an occasional third seat. The result was the DH 80A Puss Moth, which flew in March 1930.

Unfortunately Puss Moths and their occupants suffered serious accidents and several people were killed before the cause was discovered. By 1932, however, tests had proved that at high speed in turbulent conditions a wing failure could occur. Modifications included the addition of a small strut from the forward wing strut to the rear wing root fitting. Despite the bad start, the DH 80A became a popular and highly successful aeroplane with a number of achievements to its name; Australian-registered VH-UQO took 3rd place in the handicap section of the England-to-Australia Air Race in 1934, averaging 103 mph, but perhaps the most noticeable performance was by

Jim Mollison, who in 1933, flew G-ABXY from Lympne to Brazil to become the first man to fly from England to South America and the first to make a solo east-west crossing of the South Altantic.

259 Puss Moths were built between 1930 and 1933 and nearly half this number were exported.

The Exhibit: Exported new in 1931 as UN-PAX. Returned to England 1937 and registered G-AEOA. Impressed for RAF service during World War II as ES 921. Released 1946. Reconstructed while owned by Dr. J.H.B. Urmston in 1968, before purchase by A.J. Haig-Thomas as one of his famous 'Moth fleet'. On long loan to the Collection from 1978.

1930 GRANGER ARCHAEOPTERYX   Acquired 1967

Span: 27ft. 6ins.
Empty weight: 400 lbs.
Power: 32 hp Bristol Cherub flat twin.

Between the wars many individuals and small companies designed and built ultra-light aeroplanes and, although few reached the production stage, many were interesting in concept. One such machine was the diminutive Archaeopteryx, which the brothers R.F.T. and R.J.T. Granger designed, with professional help from C.H. Latimer-Needham (designer of the Luton Light aeroplanes, later the Halton Minor and others) after seeing the success of the Westland-Hill Pterodactyl in 1926. The result was a single-seater with swept-back wings and of semi-tailess layout, in that it had a fin and rudder, but no tailplane or elevators. Full-chord elevons at the wingtips, hinged near the leading edge, provided control in both roll and pitch.

The Archaeopteryx first flew at Hucknall, near Nottingham, in October 1930, but its identity belies its true age, for its registration G-ABXL was not issued until nearly two years later. Both Granger brothers flew their little machine many times locally in the Nottingham area and once ventured south as far as Hatfield for a flying display in June 1935. The throttle lever was on the outside of the fuselage, but performance on such lower power depended very much on minimum exposed frontal area and a positive rate of climb could be obtained only if the pilot's arms and elbows were tucked well into the cramped cockpit.

Tailless aeroplanes have always suffered aerodynamic problems with resulting control limitations and the Archaeopteryx must not be allowed to approach the stall. Another difficulty concerns the lack of fore-and-aft response in the take-off or landing stage, so any disturbance in pitch caused by rough ground or turbulence cannot be rectified and a landing bounce must lead to a series of bigger bounces until the airspeed decays and the aircraft stops. However, despite certain flight hazards, the idea and the design were most creditable. The Archaeopteryx was the first tractor (propeller in the front) tailless type and was a forerunner of the swept-wing machines in service today. Perhaps the Vulcan heavy bomber is the best example.

The Exhibit: G-ABXL. The only specimen built. Flown 1930-36 and then stored for 30 years before hand-over to the Collection on 28th April 1967. Restored to flying condition in Old Warden workshops and flown again in June 1971.

1932 DH 83 FOX MOTH   Loaned 1979

Span: 30ft. 10½ins.
Empty weight: 1100 lbs.
Power: 130 hp Gipsy Major I 4-cylinder inverted in-line (originally 120 hp Gipsy III)

Here we have an aeroplane that heralded a break-away in de Havilland policy, for unlike previous products which had been intended primarily as either club or private-owner machines, clearly the DH 83 had an appeal aimed at commercial operators. Behind the economy of only 120 hp the Fox Moth was capable of carrying a pilot and three passengers on medium-range journeys and, for local pleasure flights, the enclosed cabin (ahead of the pilot) could be filled to its four-seat capacity.

In its first year a specially cleaned-up Fox Moth G-ABUT enabled Wally Hope to win the King's Cup Air Race (his third win) at 124.13 mph and two years later John Grierson flew a Fox on floats via Iceland and Greenland to Ottawa. However, the type was not geared primarily to racing or records. As a workhorse it was used on scheduled airline services, mainly by the Scottish Motor Traction Company and Midland and Scottish Air Ferries, serving many remote places in the Highlands and Islands on a network of routes from Renfrew. However, the Fox became best-known for the long careers of two specimens, G-ACCB and G-ACEV, which operated from the sands of Southport to give many thousands of holidaymakers their first flights, while for six years G-ACCA and G-ACIG plied the short route between Portsmouth and Ryde on the Isle of Wight.

As with many light aircraft of the time, DH 83s found their ways into unusual places and roles; five were operated by the Brazilian Navy as navigation trainers, four (plus another home-made copy) were used by the Japan Aerial Transport Company, one served with the Spanish Air Force and two flew the air mail service in Newfoundland under the flag of Imperial Airways. World War II saw specimens impressed into service with the Air Transport Auxiliary and on radar trials duties.

Although not designed for personal pleasure, the Fox Moth was very much a pilot's aeroplane. It could ride smoothly through bumpy weather and was capable of turning on a very tight radius. However, as with so many designs of that era, it needed to be landed carefully into wind.

98 Fox Moths were built in Britain at Stag Lane and more than half were exported. As late as 1946 de Havilland Aircraft of

Canada opened a production line of an updated version powered by a Gipsy Major lc of 145 hp and 52 were sold.

The Exhibit: G-ACEJ. Built at Stag Lane, Edgware, in 1934. Used for pleasure flights from Southport sands both before and after World War II, before transfer to the Tiger Club at Redhill in 1967. Sold to A. Haig-Thomas and now on indefinite loan to the Collection.

1933 FLYING FLEA   Acquired 1967

Span: 20ft.
Empty weight: 220 lbs.
Power: Various, including Scott, Carden-Ford, Douglas Sprite, A.B.C. Scorpion and Bristol Cherub.

The Flying Flea was not intended to be a factory-produced aeroplane, for its French designer, M. Henri Mignet, aimed at the do-it-yourself market, which, though popular today in many spheres, is far from a new idea. The Flea's French name was Pou-du-Ciel, which translated literally into Sky Louse.

63

M. Mignet endeavoured to remove the characteristics of a conventional light aeroplane that were likely to be dangerous in the hands of a novice pilot who had just built his own machine. Throughout the era of flight, stalling and spinning had proved to be hazardous unknowns, so he aimed to reduce the need for control movements to an absolute minimum. By giving the wings considerable dihedral (upward curve) and placing the weight well beneath them, he dispensed with ailerons, relying wholly on pendulum stability to maintain lateral control. Fore-and-aft movement was achieved by hinging the front wing at its leading edge, so that fore-and-aft adjustment of the joystick altered the angle of incidence. There was no form of movement and no hinged surface on the rear wing or tailplane.

Although many pilots and engineers were sceptical about the practicability of these ideas, M. Mignet brought his machine to Shoreham in August 1935 and many people were highly impressed by its apparent success. The Air League took the Flea into the fold and encouraged the formation of Pou Clubs. 6000 copies of the designer's handbook were printed in English and by 1937 nearly 100 Fleas had been registered in Britain.

Unfortunately, after a bright start, the Flea ran into control problems and some of these developed into fatal accidents. The Air League recommended that the type should not be flown until the difficulties had been identified and cured; following this full-scale wind tunnel tests at Farnborough and in France indicated several serious shortcomings, with the result that the Flea failed to recover from this setback. The designer, however, insisted that the idea was sound and he developed a slightly more advanced version which flew successfully in limited numbers. One of these was built in Britain shortly after World War II.

The Exhibit: G-AEBB. Registered 1937. Early history not confirmed, but for several years after the war, was in the care of No. 124 (Southampton) Squadron of the Air Training Corps. The squadron donated it to the Collection in May 1967, since when it has been restored by A. Dowson (see Swallow on 71) of the S.V.A.S. Although technically airworthy, the Flea is not flown, but occasionally is taxied on public occasions.

1934 DH 87b HORNET MOTH   Acquired 1971

Span: 31ft. 11ins.
Empty weight: 1241 lbs.
Power: 130 hp Gipsy Major I 4-cylinder inverted in-line.

The Hornet Moth emerged in 1934 as an experimental design in an attempt to find the pattern for a modernised version of the original DH 60 Moth series. Clearly an enclosed cabin would be incorporated and side-by-side seating seemed sensible for a 'social' aeroplane. At first the DH 87 had tapered wings with almost pointed tips; these were similar to those on the DH 86 four-engined airliner that had been its immediate predecessor. Three Hornet Moths were used in a (for that time) extended testing programme lasting for a year before quantity production began.

The first batch for sale was completed in August 1935 and altogether 165 were built. However, during the development process a new, squarer wing design appeared and owners of early machines were invited to trade-in their original mainplanes for those of later layout. The change was made in order to eliminate a tendency for a wing to drop at low speed, which was considered

to be an unacceptable characteristic on a machine aimed mainly at the private-owner market. The revised version was designated DH 87b and before long all the UK-based pointed-wing specimens had disappeared.

Unlike many de Havilland designs, the Hornet Moth was not a top-line record breaker, but a comfortable mount for the executive of the day. However, it appeared in all parts of the world and examples were assembled in South Africa, Canada, Australia and India. Four were equipped with floats for Air Ministry seaplane trials at Felixstowe.

The DH 87b was less of a 'pilots aeroplane' than many de Havilland products, but it offered a good forward view, plenty of comfort and a useful range of more than 600 miles. As with the Puss Moth, the undercarriage leg fairings could be turned through ninety degrees to act as air brakes. About 8 Hornet Moths remain active in the early eighties.

The Exhibit: G-ADND. Now powered by 145 hp Gipsy Major 10. Owned for many years by P.Q. Reiss who on retirement passed it to the Air Registration Board (predecessor of today's Airworthiness Division of the CAA). Following an accident, Mr. Reiss transferred it to the Shuttleworth Collection, for whom it was rebuilt by Hawker Siddeley/British Aerospace at Chester.

1934 DH 88 COMET   Acquired 1965

Span: 44ft. 0ins.
Empty weight: 2840 lbs.
Power: 2 x 230 hp Gipsy Six R high-compression 6-cylinder inverted
in-line (but see text)

If any historic aeroplane has received well-earned publicity in the last two years or so, perhaps the de Havilland Comet of 1934 takes the lead, but this is not its first round of headline-hitting. The DH 88 was designed, built and flown in a total time of nine months to enter and win the MacRobertson Air Race in October of the same year.

That simple statement in no way expresses the magnitude of the tasks; either of producing an aeroplane with so many novel features such as a unique wooden stressed-skin construction, two-pitch propellers, a retractable undercarriage and a range of 2900 miles from tanks contained wholly within the slender fuselage, all in such record time; or of restoring a complex and incomplete aeroplane to fly again after more than 43 years on the ground in a wide range of storage conditions.

The Comet story starts with an offer — or a challenge — from Sir MacPherson Robertson, who put up £10,000 in prize money for a race from England to Australia to mark the centenary of the foundation of the State of Victoria. Most entrants planned to compete in existing aircraft types and only one company — de Havilland — was sufficiently enterprising to make positive proposals for a new design solely for the race. DH offered to produce the Comet at a highly subsidised price of £5000 for each aircraft, on condition that orders were confirmed by February 1934. In the event, three orders were received, and, by constant work day and night, the company had all three machines ready just in time to be tested and handed over prior to the deadline for appearing at the start-line at Mildenhall.

To achieve high speed, long range and accommodate a crew of two, the Comet called for considerable design ingenuity. Very clean aerodynamic lines were essential, with an absolute minimum of frontal area. To obtain both the required smoothness of form and an adequately robust structure, much of the strength was contained in the skin, which for the wings and upper and lower surfaces of the fuselage consisted of diagonally placed spruce strips. On the wings these strips, which ran at 45° to the fore and aft axis of the aircraft, were of equal width throughout but were tapered in thickness from root to tip.

Fortunately engines of the desired size and weight were available from within the de Havilland organisation. The 205 hp Gipsy Six had all six cylinders in a line and therefore offered a small frontal area, but as maximum possible power was required the basic unit was modified with an increased compression ratio and a consequent reduction in depth of the cylinder heads, therefore providing an additional 25 hp and an ability to fit tightly into small cowlings. However, in order to take off with heavy fuel loads from small airfields and yet cruise economically at the high end of the speed range, the available engine power could not be fully used with the existing patterns of propellers of fixed pitch design. Ratier, of France, had produced two-pitch propellers — fine for take-off and coarse for cruise — and these were used, although the pitch settings were not controllable from the cockpit. A bicycle pump was used to establish the fine setting before starting the engines; discs in the propeller hubs were designed to respond to air pressure when the aircraft accelerated through 140 mph after take-off, releasing the pumped-up air pressure and causing centrifugal weights to put the propellers into fully coarse pitch with a clunk. It is interesting to wonder whether both sides changed pitch at the same time!

The air race was scheduled to start at dawn on 20th October 1934. On the line at the new RAF station at Mildenhall, a host of competing types ranged from the new Douglas DC-2 and Boeing 247 airliners to a Miles Hawk from the Manawutu Aero Club of New Zealand. The three Comets were there; the black and gold G-ACSP, called 'Black Magic', owned and entered by the already famous Jim and Amy Mollison; G-ACSR, unnamed, but painted green, owned by Bernard Rubin who had engaged Owen Cathcart-Jones and Ken Waller to be his race pilots; and G-ACSS, red and white (although recently discovered DH workshop notes indicate that the white might have been silver), known as 'Grosvenor House' and entered by A.O. Edwards who was the hotel's managing director. The pilots for this were C.W.A. Scott and Tom Campbell-Black.

The story of the race warrants a book of its own. 'Black Magic' and 'Grosvenor House' each reached Baghdad non-stop, but the nameless 'SR had compass and other problems in very bad weather and the pilots were forced to make an unscheduled landing in Persia. En route, though, the fortunes changed, with 'SP retiring through repeated engine trouble; 'SR was in business again and making fast headway, but 'Grosvenor House' was just in the lead, with the KLM (Royal Dutch Airlines) DC-2 too close behind for crew comfort. All participants endured a variety of weather and technical problems, but after 70 hours and 54 minutes, G-ACSS 'Grosvenor House' was the first to cross the finishing line. The Comet qualified for both main prizes — one for speed and one for handicap — but the race rules prevented both awards going to one competitor, so the crew of 'CS opted for the main (speed) prize and the other trophy was presented to the crew of the DC-2.

The Comet was a thoroughbred aeroplane, designed and built for one purpose: to travel a long way in a short time. G-ACSR, which had finished fourth, turned round almost immediately, loaded with newreels, photographs of the winners and other valuable booty, to arrive at Lympne in Kent 13½ days after leaving Mildenhall, thus establishing an out-and-return record. G-ACSS, however, had a more leisurely journey home on board a ship; but its flying days were far from finished. As the Comet was such an advanced design, 'SS temporarily lost its bright civil colours to become K 5084 in the Royal Air Force for trials at Marlesham Heath; as such it appeared in the 1936 Pageant at Hendon. However, following a second landing accident whilst in

RAF service, it was sold as scrap, to be bought by F.E. Tasker who had it rebuilt by Essex Aero Ltd at Gravesend, where the exceptionally skilled engineer Jack Cross worked wonders both then and later. More recently Mr. Cross was actively helping with the restoration of 'CSS at Old Warden until he died towards the end of 1981.

In its new ownership G-ACSS was renamed 'The Orphan' and gained fourth place in the England to Damascus race of 1937; later in that year the same stalwart, by then called 'The Burberry' (of raincoat renown) beat the out-and-back record to the Cape, but its final acheivement was in March 1938 when it covered the 26,450 miles from England to New Zealand and home again in only 10 days, 21 hours and 22 minutes. From then on, 'SS was stored at Gravesend, where it passed much of World War II standing forlornly outside.

In addition to the three MacRobertson race participants, two later Comets were built. G-ACSP had been sold to the French Government to become F-ANPY, to be joined by a new F-ANPZ for use on high-speed mail services. The final DH 88 to leave the Hatfield factory was lost over the Sudan when the crew baled out with serious propeller problems in an attempt on the Cape record.

The Exhibit: G-ACSS. History already described. After the war years at Gravesend, restored externally by de Havilland apprentices, to be hung on exhibition in the Festival of Britain in 1951. Subsequently stored at Leavesden before hand-over as a static exhibit for the Shuttleworth Collection on 30th October

1965. In the early seventies, plans were considered for restoring this famous aeroplane to fly again; despite many problems a decision was made to go ahead and work has progressed markedly during 1981 and 1982, with technical and financial support from about 50 organisations in the aviation and allied industries. This is the most ambitious restoration task yet undertaken within the aircraft preservation movement and early in 1982 the Collection launched a public appeal for £80,000 to enable the work to be finished before the 50th anniversary of the race in October 1984. G-ACSS is on view to visitors whilst being restored.

1935 B.A. SWALLOW 2   Loaned 1978

Span: 42ft. 8½ins.
Empty weight: 990 lbs.
Power: 90 hp Pobjoy Cateract III 7 cylinder radial (some had 90 hp Cirrus Minor 4-cylinder in-line)

In 1927 the Klemm L 25 two-seat low-wing monoplane appeared in Germany as a safe and comfortable mount for private owners. Despite its Salmson radial engine of only 75 hp., the type proved popular immediately and soon specimens were delivered to Britain.

The L 25 owed its success to a low wing loading, docile handling qualities and a reliable engine. By 1933 Major E.F. Stephen, the UK agent, had imported and sold 27 aircraft before establishing the British Klemm Aeroplane Company to build these machines at Hanworth. The British-built version differed little from the German original, but the airframe was strengthened in a few parts and after the first six machines, the production power unit was changed from the Salmson to the Pobjoy Cateract, which offered an additional 15 hp. By 1935, however, some redesign work had been completed, to square-off the wing-tips, rudder, tailplane and fuselage top-decking for ease of quantity construction; the result became known as Swallow 2. New finance was injected into the business and the UK firm became the British Aircraft Manufacturing Company.

The 42nd airframe to be built in Britain used the Blackburn Cirrus Minor 4-cylinder inverted in-line engine and, from that point onward, a roughly equal number of Swallows left the line with this and with the Cateract. These aircraft were built essentially for the British home market, for 98 out of 105 produced at Hanworth were acquired by flying clubs or private owners in this country. Not surprisingly, a leading user of the Cirrus-powered Swallow was the Blackburn Aircraft Co., which operated 15 on No. 4 Elementary and Reserve Flying School at Brough in East Yorkshire.

Unlike many civil light aircraft in common use in the late thirties, in general Swallows were not impressed into active flying service in World War II. One flew as a glider at Farnborough, but the majority suffered the relative indignity of being used as ground instructional airframes. Despite (or perhaps because of?) this, 17 Swallow 2s survived to fly again shortly after the war. Today one Klemm L 25 and 2 B.A. Swallows remain in flying condition.

The uncowled radial is heavily geared-down between the engine and propeller and the sound is unmistakable.

The Exhibit: G-AFCL. Built November 1937 and registered to W.L. Hope. Owned immediately after World War II by G.H. Forsaith, who based it at Thruxton. To Bert Etheridge (wood craftsman at Old Warden) in May 1965. Owned and restored for the Collection by A. Dowson, a member of the Shuttleworth Veteran Aeroplane Society.

1935 PERCIVAL D.3 GULL   Acquired 1961

Span: 36ft. 2ins.
Empty weight: 1500 lbs.
Power: 200 hp Gipsy Six I 6-cylinder inverted in-line.

The Gull is an example of an aercplane that is difficult to date (see appendix III), for the original machine that flew first in 1932 was a substantially different aircraft from the variant that emerged two years later. The earlier version was built under contract by George Parnall and Co. Ltd. of Yate, near Bristol (see Parnall Elf on 57) and this had either the 160 hp Napier Javelin or 130 hp Gipsy Major as a power source. By 1934, however, the Percival Aircraft Co. Ltd., had its own factory at Gravesend and from here the design developed with a neater, single-strut undercarriage and eventually boasted the additional performance offered by the 200 hp Gipsy Six engine. The exhibit in the Collection is one of these later machines, built in 1935.

As with all Percival aircraft of the time, the Gull range was designed by and built under the supervison of E.W. Percival, who carried out the first flight of the prototype in 1932 and flew it in the King's Cup Air Race of that same year. At one stage the

company used a series of type numbers that continued into the post-war era of the Provost, Prince and Pembroke, but these had been retrospectively allocated to the machines of the thirties and a 'P' designation was wrongly attributed to the Gull-Six.

An early Gull-Four flew from Lympne in Kent, (now closed) to Darwin, Australia in the hands of Sir Charles Kingsford Smith, to arrive on 10th December 1933 after 7 days, 4 hours and 44 minutes. In 1935, Edgar Percival flew a Gull Six from Gravesend to Algeria and back in a day, while shortly afterwards Jean Batten began her series of record-breaking activities, starting with the first flight across the South Altantic by a woman pilot that enabled her to reach Brazil in 2 days, 13 hours and 15 minutes after leaving Lympne. For this she was awarded the C.B.E. In the following year she set course for Australia and reached Darwin from England in 5 days, 21 hours and 3 minutes. She extended this to complete the first-ever flight from England to New Zealand. The return flight from Darwin to Lympne was achieved in 2 hours 48 minutes less than on the outward journey.

The basic Gull was developed into the more sophisticated four-seat Vega Gull, which in turn formed the basis for the Percival Proctor of RAF radio-training and communications renown. One other Gull-Six and three Proctors remain in flying condition in 1982.

The Exhibit: G-ADPR. Built September 1935. The machine was used by Jean Batten for all her record flights. Impressed into wartime RAF service as AX 866 and later bought back by the Percival Aircraft Co. Ltd., whose Directors (by then Hunting Percival) passed it to the Collection on 25th April 1961.

1935 DH 90 DRAGONFLY   Loaned 1982

Span: 43ft. 0ins.
Empty weight: 2500 lbs.
Power: 2 x 130 hp DH Gipsy Major I inverted in-line.

The last of the long line of de Havilland biplanes, the DH 90 Dragonfly must have been one of the first-ever designs to cater specifically for the serious executive market. Business and tycoon-owned twins are relatively commonplace in the eighties, but in the mid-thirties aircraft with more than one engine were engaged primarily on airline or charter work. That the Dragonfly filled the small need for this market, at the then high price of

£2,650, is indicated by the names of some of the owners of the time: Lord Beaverbrook, Loel Guinness, Sir Philip Sassoon and King Feisal of Iraq. However, other DH 90s were used for more workaday purposes, with four operated by the Royal Canadian Mounted Police to check rum running.

The Dragonfly differed structurally from the basic box of the DH 89 Rapide, in that the later aircraft had a monocoque shell of pre-formed ply stiffened with light spruce stringers. By using very strong wingspars in the lower section inboard of the engines, external bracing wires were eliminated and this provided a clearway between the wings and fuselage for executives to enter and leave the cabin. The DH 90 seated a pilot and four passengers, one of whom sat in the front. Because of its clean lines, the lower-powered Gipsy Major engines were able to provide the Dragonfly with a climb and cruise performance broadly comparable with that of the Rapide and, because of the lower fuel consumption, a better basic range. However, only 21 were sold to British customers, the remaining 46 serving in various parts of the world for a variety of purposes, including use as communications machines by the Swedish and Danish Air Forces.

14 Dragonflies were impressed for service in World War II and a few made brief subsequent appearances as civil machines. The last in Britain was G-AETD, flown by the North Altantic route to the Tallmantz Collection in California in August 1964.

The Exhibit: Formerly ZS-CTR and CR-AAB. No original British registration. Now G-AEDU, but not the first DH 90 destined to carry this identity, as the original 'DU was re-allocated the letters G-ADXM. Unused for 45 years, G-AEDU was re-allocated to this aircraft by the Civil Aviation Authority to enable it to carry markings appropriate to its year of manufacture. Returned to this country in 1980 and extensively overhauled. One of the exhibits in the de Havilland Flying Centre at Old Warden.

1937 DH 94 MOTH MINOR   Loaned 1979

Span: 36ft. 7ins.
Empty weight: 983 lbs.
Power: 90 hp Gipsy Minor 4-cylinder inverted in-line.

For many years Geoffrey (later Sir Geoffrey) de Havilland had strong personal views about the improved performance that would be possible from a cantilever monoplane, compared with all the drag created by struts and wires of most aircraft in production in the early thirties. In fact, as early as 1931, the DH 81 Swallow Moth had been built to this 'clean' specification, but was shelved to concentrate on series production of established Moth variants. However, he persisted and on 22nd June 1937 he made the first flight in the prototype DH 90 Moth Minor, which became G-AFRD.

The Moth Minor reverted to the basic spruce and plywood fuselage structure used on the earliest Moths, with plywood-covered wings with box spars; the wings folded from the front spar of the centre section. It cruised comfortably at 100 mph on the economy of only 90hp and, at £575 ex works, proved popular with flying clubs and private owners. Although basically an

open-cockpit design, a hinged-top coupé version appeared by 1938. Unlike the majority of tandem two-seaters of the time, the DH 94 was flown solo from the front seat.

Through no fault of the design, the Moth Minor's production was quickly curtailed. Just over 100 had been completed on the outbreak of World War II and as the British factory facilities were needed for military machinery, the drawings, jigs, tools and unfinished Minors were sent by ship to Australia where about 40 were completed at de Havilland's Bankstown factory for the Royal Australian Air Force.

Several Moth Minors survived the war and G-AFOJ achieved 137.5 mph in the 1950 Daily Express air race, flown by Pat Fillingham, who at the time was DH's chief production test pilot. Another, G-AFNI, performed less dramatically with the Community Flying Club at Woodley (now closed) near Reading; in 1949 the author took his father in this machine for his one and only flight. Apart from the machine now at Old Warden, two DH 94s are known to exist in complete condition.

The Exhibit: G-AFNG. Constructor's No. 94014. Owned in 1939 by Cambridge Aero Club and impressed during World War II as AW 112. First post-war owner was D. Cotter, who based it at White Waltham. Coupé conversion in 1954. Now owned by Antony Haig Thomas and loaned to the Collection to form a part of the de Havilland Centre.

Chapter 5
Military Aircraft after
World War I

The development of military aircraft has been a start-and-stop operation throughout the history of Service aviation. This has been dictated almost entirely by the degree of urgency for an effective fighting force and the directly-related funds that were available. After rapid progress throughout the 1914-18 war, culminating in such effective operational types as the Bristol Fighter, SE5a and, ultimately, the Sopwith Snipe, the military flying machine made virtually no progress for about a decade. Numbers of aircraft, too, fell dramatically, from a total of 22,647 on RAF strength (with 188 operational squadrons) at the time of the Armistice to a mere twelve first-line squadrons by the end of 1919.

Although the following years saw a slow growth again in numerical strength, there was little sign of really new equipment. One squadron of Snipes served as Great Britain's only fighter defence until late in 1922 and despite its outdated rotary engine the type remained on first-line strength until eight years after the war. The ubiquitous Bristol Fighter saw extended service on numerous duties, especially army co-operation, for fourteen years of post-armistice peace, while the trainer version served with Oxford and Cambridge University Air Squadrons well into the thirties. The Avro 504, too, enjoyed a long life; its post-war development, from the rotary-engined K variant to the 504N with an Armstrong-Siddeley Lynx static radial, proved the rightness of the original design as well as indicating the financially frugal atmosphere prevailing at the time. In 1931 504Ns pioneered the art of serious tuition in instrument flying and remained in use at flying training schools until finally replaced in 1933, mainly by the Avro Tutor from the same stable.

Because of the long service provided by these 1914-18 designs, readers will not be surprised to find a gap of ten years between the end of hostilities and the date of the first true post-war military type to be represented in the Collection. Even this was a trainer, in the form of the little Hawker Tomtit that was one of two machines to compete for the task of replacing the Avro 504N. Also, visitors to Old Warden are able to see the larger Avro Tutor, which was the Tomtit's rival that eventually won the main production contract for the RAF. More surprising to many, though, will be the fact that the de Havilland Tiger Moth, known mainly as an elementary trainer used in large numbers during World War II, entered service before the Tutor and served briefly at No. 3 Flying Training School during 1932 before the Tutor replaced it. Several years later this process was reversed!

Throughout the period of peace in the twenties and most of the thirties, relatively few real changes emerged either in the basic design layouts of the aircraft in use or in the roles that they performed. On the operational side, perhaps the long line of Hawker biplanes that served so well as fighters, light bombers, army co-operation and general duties machines typified the commonality of the military flying scene of the time. All were strut-braced biplanes, with fixed undercarriages, open cockpits, and all, except the single-seat Fury, accommodated two in tandem; they had fixed-pitch propellers and other basic features that had applied to most types designed and produced during the earlier war. In most cases bombs were hung externally, radio of any sort was an exception rather than the rule and armament remained thin; even the Fury fighter had only two guns whilst the Hind general-purpose light bomber of late 1935 retained the World War I practice of one fixed forward-firing Vickers and one movable Lewis machine gun. The main progress in nearly twenty years related to steady increases in power, with the Rolls-Royce Kestrels of both the Fury and Hind producing 640 hp compared with the 275 hp of the Rolls-Royce Falcon in the 1917 Bristol Fighter. The latter and the Hind make interesting comparisions; both can be studied on a tour of the Old Warden hangars.

By the mid-thirties more positive signs of progress started to emerge. The Gloster Gladiator single-seat fighter serves as a prime preserved example to show the change from the traditional to the new; although a biplane with a fixed undercarriage, the production Gladiator (which entered service in February 1937 with No. 72 Squadron) had an effective armament of four fixed guns, an enclosed cockpit with a sliding canopy and wing flaps. In some ways it boasted many of the features of the future that were to be found on the Hurricanes and Spitfires which followed the Gladiator into service, to make it the RAF's last-ever biplane fighter.

The change from the strut-braced biplane to the cantilever monoplane, on which all the structural strength was contained within the airframe, with need for neither struts nor bracing wires, called for a trainer of similar layout. So from Air Ministry specification T. 40/36 came the Miles Magister, an open cockpit tandem two-seat low-wing monoplane with spilt flaps, a tailwheel, brakes, blind-flying hood and clearance for all normal aerobatic manoeuvres. Ironically, this machine that was so modern in appearance moved backwards in one sense, for gradually, beneath the visible surface, the long line of traditional biplanes produced between the wars had changed in construction materials and methods from all-wood to mainly metal structures. The Magister was all wood, as was its bigger and more powerful brother, the Master advanced trainer.

In a comparatively short time the biplane almost disappeared from the Service scene, but there were a few exceptions; The Tiger Moth continued in use as an elementary trainer until after World War II, the Dominie twin-engine radio trainer and communications machine (a military variant of the Dragon-Rapide short-haul airliner) lasted almost as long and the Swordfish naval torpedo-carrier seemed to go on for ever.

The big change, however, had come to stay — and had come with a rush. Monoplane bombers such as the Fairey Battle, Bristol Blenheim and Vickers Wellington and their fighter counterparts in the Hawker Hurricane and Supermarine Spitfire, entered squadron service within a few months of each other in 1937 and 1938. Alas, many of these types that saw active service in the early part of the war, together with later designs such as the Handley-Page Halifax and Short Stirling heavy bombers, have not survived into the present era of aircraft preservation. In the main, and understandably, the larger the type the less is the likehood that it would be saved from the scrap-man's axe; but the Hurricane and the Spitfire remain with us today and specimens have been preserved by the Shuttleworth Collection. The Hurricane — an early Canadian-built Mark I that operated from a merchant ship in 1941 — is the oldest specimen of the type that will fly again and is on a long-term restoration programme (see

Appendix I) in conjunction with the Imperial War Museum at Duxford. The Collection has a pair of Spitfires; a Mark Vc that flies regularly and a photo-reconnaissance Mark XI that is undergoing a rebuild by a volunteer crew.

As the Shuttleworth Collection aims to show the earlier days of the development of the flying machine, Word War II has been selected as a broad cut-off point. Many other collections contain aircraft of the post 1939-45 period, so the Trustees consider that to duplicate these efforts would weaken the limited resources at Old Warden that are available for tending the needs of the true veterans. However, as there is no other preserved range of elementary/basic trainers that have been used by the flying Services since military aviation began in 1910, Old Warden's hangars house post-war types such as the 1950 de Havilland Chipmunk and Percival Provost of 1953 in order to make the unique collection complete.

The Chipmunk, in particular, has a special claim to fame, for despite the much-acclaimed records of long service for both the Avro 504 series and the Tiger Moth, it has beaten both by very considerable margins and in 1980 re-entered regular RAF use as a primary trainer. The Chipmunks now operating are thirty or more years of age and, on present plans, they are destined to serve for another decade or more. Only the de Havilland Devon communications aircraft has served for longer, but this is likely to be phased-out first.

The end of World War II saw the most dramatic change in the characteristics of military aircraft. Although the Gloster Meteor jet fighter saw limited operational service in 1945, the other types in service were piston-engined, nearly all with traditional tailwheel undercarriages and other features that were soon to be lost for ever. Handling and operating techniques changed, with the newer types generally easier to fly (no swing on take-off with a jet, whereas this was a major feature on powerful piston-powered machines) but more tricky to operate, mainly because of very high fuel consumption at low levels.

So there are several reasons supporting the Shuttleworth Collection's policy to use the 1939-45 war as the end of an era in the history of the military flying machine. The aircraft to be seen at Old Warden form a unique range and most of the aeroplanes on display are the World's sole surviving flying examples of their types. This adds to the significance of the exhibition; also it increases the value of a long and detailed study of the aircraft that are described in the pages that follow.

1928 HAWKER TOMTIT   Acquired 1956

Span: 28ft. 6ins.
Empty weight: 1100 lbs.
Power: 150 hp Armstrong-Siddeley Mongoose 111c 5-cylinder radial.

As the Avro 504 series enjoyed such a long and successful career in the training role, the Royal Air Force had no requirement for a new trainer for twelve years after the end of World War I. In fact, very few new military aircraft of any type appeared during this quiet period in the twenties and the Tomtit was unusual in several ways. It was a completely new design, which became the first in the long line of Hawker military biplanes that were the mainstays of all but the heavy bomber and transport squadrons in the thirties. Although the better-known Hart light bomber flew first in prototype form, the Tomtit was ahead in initial issue to RAF units.

The Tomtit was one of the pace-setters in the changeover from wooden to metal construction, with a steel tube fuselage of a pattern that became the Hawker norm as far ahead as the Hurricane. Other salient features included wing slats, a blind-flying hood and a heavily staggered wing layout to permit rapid exit by parachute. There were no brakes, but the pupil's seat was adjustable for height. An unusual cockpit characteristic was the absence of a nut for adjusting throttle friction and yet the setting seemed to be suitable for all taxying and flight conditions.

In 1929 Tomtits were issued to No. 3 Flying Training School at Grantham (Spitalgate) and to the Central Flying School at Wittering. A Tomtit on the strength of No. 24 (Communications) Squadron at Northolt was flown regularly by the then Prince of Wales. The type was withdrawn from RAF service in 1935 and several were sold to civilian owners, to join a small number that had been built for the civil market and which did not see Service use. Tomtits were built also for the Royal Canadian and Royal New Zealand Air Forces.

The Tomtit is tail-light on the ground, but apart from a poor roll-rate with ailerons on the lower wings only, it is a delight to

fly. Although a well-loved aeroplane among the relatively small number of sporting pilots who flew it in the thirties, a succession of entries in air races produced disappointing results.

Six Tomtits were flying at the outbreak of War in 1939 and all became camouflaged although, unusually, they remained civil registered for use on communications duties.

The Exhibit: K 1786/G-AFTA. The last Tomtit built and the only survivor. Flown as a 'hack' during World War II by Alex Henshaw of pre-war Mew Gull fame, who temporarily fitted a Spitfire windscreen. Later used by R.G. Stafford Allen, often for glider towing. Purchased by Neville Duke, then Hawkers' chief test pilot, who flew it in many races and displays. Purchased by Hawker Aircraft in 1950 to form the Hawker house trio (with the Hurricane and Hart), before hand over to the Shuttleworth Collection in 1956. In 1966 was repainted by Hawker-Siddeley at Dunsfold from a dark blue and gold scheme to its original Service markings.

1931 DH 82 TIGER MOTH   Acquired 1966

Span: 29ft. 4ins.
Empty weight: 1090 lbs.
Power: Originally 120 hp DH Gipsy III, but later 130 hp Gipsy Major I 4-cylinder inverted in-line.

The DH 82 Tiger Moth is an earlier aeroplane than many people realise, for the prototype flew in October 1931. Although a few early production machines filtered from the factory at Stag Lane (later Hatfield) directly onto the civilian market, by far the majority served with the RAF or with the Elementary and Reserve Flying Schools; at that time, aircraft on these units carried civil registrations as they were owned by the companies that operated them under contract to the Air Ministry. In practice, therefore, the Tiger Moth was essentially an aeroplane earning its keep for Service purposes.

Developed from the DH 60 G Gipsy Moth, the DH 82 Tiger Moth was strengthened for Service use, incorporated an inverted rather than upright engine (which provided an improved forward view) and had the wings staggered for ease of exit by parachute. After initial experience with the type, the Air Ministry ordered several modifications, including the Gipsy Major engine instead of the Gipsy III and plywood instead of fabric-covered fuselage

top decking. This became the DH 82 A Tiger Moth II, which remained the standard variant for the remainder of the type's history.

By 1937, spare production capacity enabled de Havilland to produce Tiger Moths in quantity for civil use. These were needed to replace a host of ageing types then in use with the flying clubs, but this was a relatively short lease of new life, for with war starting only two years later all the machines on the lines were required for Service use. Then the Hatfield production facilities became fully committed to produce the Mosquito, so in 1941 Tiger Moth manufacture was transferred to Morris Motors at Cowley, near Oxford. In the same year, fuselage strakes were fitted to overcome difficulties with spin recovery.

Before, during and shortly after World War II the Tiger Moth was actively employed as the main elementary trainer for Service pilots. Nearly 7300 were built, including large numbers in Canada, Australia and New Zealand. Although replaced by Prentices in regular units by 1948, DH 82s continued to serve with Reserve Flying Schools and University Air Squadrons until superceded by Chipmunks in 1950-51. Since then, the Tiger Moth has remained a popular possession among sporting pilots and in the past decade its market value has increased each year; yet at the end of World War II, the Air Ministry disposed of hundreds in fly-away condition at £100 each, with a specially-arranged concession price of £50 if purchased by a recognised flying club. Some were sold for only £25 apiece.

The Tiger Moth was the last trainer to require pilots to fly in the traditional manner, taxying without the benefits of brakes, needing considerable use of rudder to maintain balanced flight, especially in turns, and generally flying largely by feel or, as it was termed 'by the seat of the pants'. Today three flying clubs operate DH 82 As, but only the Cambridge Flying Group provides basic instruction for beginners. Altogether about 45 Tiger Moths are flying in Britain and one, G-AIVW, operates on floats as the Sea Tiger.

The Exhibit: T 6818/G-ANKT. Three Tiger Moths were acquired by the Collection in various states of disrepair, but the fuselage and most main components are from 'NKT. The rebuild was carried out almost entirely by two former engineering apprentices at Old Warden. First flight in Shuttleworth ownership was on 3rd October 1977.

1931 AVRO TUTOR

Acquired 1959

Span: 34ft.
Empty weight: 1800 lbs.
Power: 240 hp. Armstrong-Siddeley Lynx IVc 7-cylinder radial.

The Tutor is difficult to date, for although the production version and the name appeared in 1931, a basically similar prototype known as the Avro Trainer, with an Armstrong-Siddeley Mongoose, had appeared in the new aircraft park at the RAF Pageant in 1930. A few Trainers served in the RAF for evaluation purposes alongside the similarly-powered Hawker Tomtit, but the later Lynx-engined Tutor became the standard production variant.

Tutors replaced Avro 504Ns at the Central Flying School, which worked-up an impressive formation aerobatic act with six aircraft that were painted with red and white stripes on the upper surfaces of the top wings to accentuate their inverted performances. From 1933 until 1936 this act became a regular and much-admired feature of the Hendon Pageants. On more routine duties Tutors served with the Royal Air Force College at Cranwell and with Nos. 3 and 5 Flying Training Schools at Grantham and Sealand respectively. At Grantham, the type replaced Tiger Moths, which surprisingly had entered service a short time previously as 504N replacements.

The Tutor was a luxurious and well-equipped aeroplane for its time, with a tailwheel, effective brakes, seats that could be adjusted for height and rudder pedals for distance, unusually spacious cockpits and a variable incidence tailplane. With ailerons on upper and lower wings, control was positive with good roll response. Perhaps it was a little docile as a trainer; certainly it required less attention to detail than the Tiger Moth, although the Tutor's large radial engine must have been useful as an exercise in teaching the operation of more powerful motors.

In addition to the standard production machines, between 1934 and 1936 14 Tutors were produced as floatplanes for use by the Seaplane Training Flight at Calshot and a developed Tutor variant, the Avro 626, entered service in small numbers in 1935 with the Air Navigation School at Andover. This was given the name Prefect and although civil 626s retained the Lynx engine, those for the RAF were fitted with 277 hp Cheetahs.

Primarily a military aeroplane, only 19 Tutors appeared on the civil register and three were equipped with survey cameras to map large areas of Tanganyika. The type was used also by Air Service Training at Hamble. Of the later 626 and 637 variants, 17 held British registrations and several were exported to Hong Kong.

Three ex-RAF Tutors survived World War II, but by 1949 one had succumbed to the effects of age and another was lost in an accident following an engine failure.

The Exhibit: K3215/G-AHSA. The world's sole surviving Tutor. One of the main RAF production batch built in 1933. Served with the RAF College, Cranwell, 1933-36 and then with the Central Flying School. Later used on communications duties and believed to be the last Tutor on RAF strength when struck-off as late as December 1946. Privately owned at Burnaston, Derby by Wing Cmdr. Heywood and suffered crankshaft failure on a ground-run for the film "Reach for the Sky", when it was purchased by the Collection. The engine subsequently used was built-up by Armstrong-Siddeley at Coventry from the best components of three non-working units including one in the museum of the College of Aeronautics at Cranfield. Engine problems in 1979 caused the machine to be grounded for a considerable time, but as a world-wide search failed to find a

suitable Lynx, the existing engine was painstakingly rebuilt at Old Warden in 1981-82 by a senior member of the engineering staff.

1933 CIERVA C 30 A   Acquired 1954
1934 AVRO ROTA

Rotor diameter: 37ft. 0ins.
Empty weight: 1270 lbs.
Power: 140 hp Armstrong-Siddeley Genet Major 1 A 7-cylinder radial.

Don Juan de la Cierva, who is credited with inventing the first practical rotating wing, brought his first autogiro to the UK from his native Spain in 1925 at the invitation of the Air Ministry. This, the C.6A, was basically an Avro 504K without its mainplanes and fitted with a 4-bladed rotor on a steel tube pylon. A developed version, the C.6D, still based on the 504, became the first two-seat autogiro, flying for the first time from Hamble in July 1926.

The rotors on Cierva's machines were not driven by or connected to the engine, but relied for their rotation wholly on a forward airspeed; hence the name autogiro. Not surprisingly there were many development problems and a number of crashes, but each difficulty was thoroughly investigated and a long research programme continued; during this time various one-off variants were produced to Cierva's designs by the A.V. Roe, de Havilland and Comper companies, with a production batch of 15 C. 19s built at Hamble. The Autogiro Flying School operated from Hanworth, now swamped in the empire known as London Airport (Heathrow).

The autogiro came into its own with the design of the C 30A. The earlier machines had used movable flying control surfaces on the same principle as a conventional aeroplane, the C. 19 having ailerons, elevator and rudders. This had resulted in the benefits of the inherent slow flying qualities, with scope for nearly vertical landing approaches, to be largely negated because these controls became progressively less effective as airspeed decreased. With the C. 30 A, however, a tilting rotor head with a control column hanging down from it provided control movements in all three axes; when the column was moved sideways for a turn, the machine assumed the correct bank angle.

By this time the Royal Air Force was interested in the use of the autogiro for army co-operation duties. Between August 1934 and

May 1935 twelve Cierva C 30As were built for the Service under contract by A.V. Roe and Co. Ltd at Manchester and, known as the Avro Rota, were based initially at Old Sarum. With the outbreak of war in 1939, these Rotas were joined by a number of impressed civil C. 30 As, the type serving briefly at Duxford, and later at Halton and Henley. No. 529 Squadron was the only full autogiro squadron in the RAF, but the Rotas remained in use until the end of hostilities in 1945 when the unit was disbanded.

12 Cierva C. 30 As survived the war for sale as surplus at RAF Kemble, but few were used again to any extent, although the Fairey Aviation Co. operated three for brief experiments and to gain rotary-wing experience while building the prototype Fairey Gydrodyne helicopter. The last airworthy specimen, G-AHTZ (which had been G-ACUI before the war, HM 581 in wartime, and should have been re-issued with its original registration) was burned in an accident at Elmdon Airport, Birmingham, in 1958.

The Exhibit: K 4234/G-AHMJ. Built as an Avro Rota for the RAF in 1934. Registered to Fairey Aviation in July 1946 and disposed of to Hayes and Harlington Sea Cadets a year later. Transferred to the Shuttleworth Collection in 1954, stored for many years and later restored to exhibition condition by SVAS member Ken Hyde and partner. Loaned to the Army Corps Museum at Middle Wallop during 1982.

1934 DH 89 A DRAGON RAPIDE   Loaned 1982
1938 DH 89 B (LATER DOMINIE) (but see text)

Span: 48ft. 0ins.
Empty weight: 3,230 lbs.
Power: Initially 2 x 200 hp DH Gipsy Six inverted in-line but later 2 x 205 hp DH Gipsy Queen 3.

Once again dating problems come to the fore. The first de Havilland D.H. 89 Dragon Six flew on 17th April 1934, to be renamed Dragon Rapide on entering production later that year. The designation DH 89 A came two years later, with the fitting of trailing edge flaps and the more modern Gipsy Queen engines. The name Dominie for the military variant was not adopted until 1941, despite the fact that the first DH 89 had entered RAF service as early as 1935.

For all practical purposes the Rapide (the prefix Dragon was soon dropped) and the Dominie are identical aircraft, with the former wearing civil registrations and the other carrying Service numbers. Civil Rapides were introduced extensively from the mid-thirites, replacing the earlier DH 84 Dragons on most of the internal and shot-haul air routes. Main airline operators included Hillman Airways and Railway Air Services, with the latter operating a fleet of eight between Croydon, Speke (Liverpool), Renfrew (Edinburgh) and Belfast, adding Whitchurch (Bristol), Eastleigh (Southampton) and Shoreham into the summer scheduled circuits. On the charter side, companies such as Olley Air Service flew Rapides all over Europe and the near East. Others performed as navigation trainers for Airwork, while further afield Rapides patrolled the Iraq Petroleum Company's desert pipelines. Wherever there was a task for a reliable workhorse, the Rapide was there.

On the Service side, the Rapide competed under specification 18/35 for a requirement for a Coastal Reconnaissance aircraft; an armed example, K4772, was given extensive military trials, but the contract was awarded to A.V. Roe and the rugged Anson Mk I. Six Rapides were delivered to the RAF for communications duties in 1938 and 1939, but quantity production for Service use almost coincided with the outbreak of war, with considerable numbers built as radio trainers.

Dominies fufilled several roles and in addition to extensive service with the RAF they were operated by the Fleet Air Arm and the Air Transport Auxiliary. As with the Tiger Moth, de

Havilland's manufacturing facilities at Hatfield were required for Mosquitoes, so from 1942 onward Dominies were built by Brush Coachworks at Loughborough, in Leicestershire, where the type remained in production until mid-1946.

After the war, the DH 89 A again became a familiar sight on short-haul air services. The largest fleet, of mixed pre-war Rapides and demobbed Dominies, was operated by British European Airways on the Scottish routes and to the Channel and Scilly Islands. In 1950, 18 were in use, known collectively as the 'Islander' class. Many smaller operators used Rapides on both charter and scheduled services, with Derby Airways (predecessor of today's British Midland Airways) serving the centre of England on a service from Derby, Wolverhampton and Birmingham to the Channel Islands. The DH 89 A was an interesting aeroplane to fly, with a very basic cabin for the pilot only in the extreme nose, much of it surrounded by the bare stringers and fabric. The forward view was excellent; the ailerons were heavy, but positive and powerful, and more than one pilot has described the handling as being comparable with two Tiger Moths strapped together!

By 1982 only four Rapides remained in flying condition in Britain, mainly in private ownership as preserved historic aeroplanes, but one lone specimen operates commercially on pleasure flights, mainly capturing the crowds at flying displays.

The Exhibit: Z 7260/G-AHGD. Owned by Michael Astor. Until 1982 based at Wycombe Air Park, but transferred to Old Warden as an exhibit in the de Havilland Flying Centre. Finished as a war-time ambulance aircraft and named 'Women of the Empire'.

1934 HAWKER HIND. Acquired 1971

Span: 37ft. 3ins.
Empty weight: 3250 lbs.
Power: 640 hp Rolls-Royce Kestrel V 12-cylinder liquid-cooled Vee

Without the long line of Hawker military biplanes that served in the thirties, the backbone of the Royal Air Force would have been very thin. With the ubiquitous Hart and its descendants fulfilling almost every role in almost every sphere, the Fury as a single-seat fighter, the Demon as a two-seat fighter, the Audax on army co-operation, the Hardy on general duties and the Hind as an all-purpose day bomber, all were powered by various versions of the Rolls-Royce Kestrel and all were broadly similar in appearance. Of all the Hawker types of the period that served with the RAF only the first — the relatively small Tomtit trainer of 1928 — and the last — the Hector of 1936 which was an Audax replacement — were powered by engines other than the Kestrel.

The Hind entered the arena when the Hawker biplane series was well matured and in the early days of the RAF's pre-war expansion scheme. The prototype took to the air on 12th September 1934 and the first production machine, for No. 21 squadron at Bircham Newton, flew almost exactly a year later. Altogether 528 Hinds were built and these replaced Harts on nearly all first-line light bomber units, as well as forming the equipment for several new squadrons in a rapidly-growing air force.

The Hind differed from its predecessor in having more than 100 additional hp from its supercharged Kestrel, a tailwheel in place of a skid (although later Hart Trainers had wheels), a more developed exhaust system and a cut-away rear cockpit to provide a better view for the gunner.

The last Hinds were replaced in front-line squadrons in the UK shortly before the start of World War II, but about 140 were converted — and 20 built — as dual-control advanced trainers to join and sometimes replace the 500 Hart trainers that had been supplied previously; some of these served into the early forties. The author remembers seeing six of these aircraft, camouflaged, of course, by contrast with the pre-war silver finish, operated by the Air Transport Auxiliary at White Waltham as late as 1942. They were hidden in an orchard and taxied across a road to the aerodrome before and after flight. Oversea, Hart variants were used in many places and in many roles, especially on the north-west frontiner in India, with two batches of Hinds delivered to the Royal Afghan Air Force: the first with 8 new aircraft in 1938 and two years later 10 ex-RAF machines. Almost certainly the last of the Hart variants to serve in Britain in numbers (although a few odd specimens survived as "hacks") were Hectors used for towing Hotspur training gliders. The last few of these were

withdrawn and replaced by Masters early in 1943. The Afghans, however, continued to operate their Hinds until 1956.

The Exhibit: One of the machines delivered new to the Royal Afghan Air Force in 1938. Presented to the Shuttleworth Collection and retrieved overland on a journey of 6000 miles with transport supplied by the Ford Motor Company. Subsequently restored in the Old Warden workshops to fly for the first time in a quarter of a centry on 17th August 1981. Made its first public appearance in the air, resplendent in Afghan markings, on 25th October 1981. Now one of the most popular performers in the Collection.

1934 GLOSTER GLADIATOR   Acquired 1960

Span: 32ft. 3ins.
Empty weight: 3450 lbs.
Power: 840 hp Bristol Mercury IX 9-cylinder radial

The Gladiator was the last in the line of inter-war Gloster fighters — following the Grebe, Gamecock and Gauntlet — to become the RAF's final biplane fighter. The type started as an unnamed private venture and in this form flew as early as September 1934, to be followed by an order for 23 aircraft placed in July of the following year. The machines ordered for RAF service differed from the earlier prototype in having enclosed cockpits with sliding hoods and a more developed mark of Mercury.

In its production form, to Air Ministry specification 14/35, the Gladiator entered front-line service with No. 72 Squadron in February 1937 and with No. 3 Squadron a month later. Before the initial deliveries were made, a further 180 had been ordered and success was such that manufacture continued until April 1940, by which time nearly 500 had been built for British use and about 240 had been delivered to nine overseas air forces.

The Gladiator was both the last of the old and the first of the new. By the late thirties, a biplane with a fixed undercarriage had a short life expectation as an operational aeroplane, but the enclosed cockpit, flaps and four .303m Browning machine guns providing twice the fire power of its predecessors gave it a logical place in the move towards the monoplane. Clearly Gladiators were obsolescent as fighters by the beginning of World War II, but they served gallantly in many spheres and formed the

equipment of No. 247 Squadron to defend the naval dockyard at Plymouth in the Battle of Britain. Their most publicly-acclaimed wartime exploits were the operations from a frozen lake in Norway and the defence of Malta, but later they continued to serve in small numbers on second-line duties, particularly on meteorological reconnaissance work. The author remembers seeing a camouflaged Gladiator at White Waltham and another visiting Hawkers' airfield at Langley as late as the end of 1944.

With 253 mph as its published top speed (always a design figure that eludes anyone who flies any type) the Gladiator depended mainly on its impressive manoeuvrability to succeed operationally; certainly in an unhostile environment that enables the lone cockpit occupant to enjoy the pure pleasures of flight, the Gladiator excelled as a flying machine and those of us who have been privileged to take the air in the Collection's preserved specimen will not forget either its impressive handling features or the associated atmosphere that provides such ample scope for an imaginative mind.

The Exhibit: L8032/G-AMRK. Manufactured in 1938. The world's only airworthy Gladiator. Built-up to flying condition in 1948 by Vivian Bellamay at Eastleigh, Southampton and flown under civil markings. Passed to the Gloster Aircraft Company and extensively rebuilt at Hucclecote during the early fifties; guns were fitted and the aircraft was repainted in Service markings. When Gloster Aircraft closed down, presented by Hawker Siddeley to the Collection for safe keeping in November 1980. For a time it flew with the incorrect serial K8032 to represent a machine on the strength of 72 Squadron. A second, incomplete Gladiator (parts of which were used in the original post-war rebuild) is owned by the Collection and is on long loan to the Royal Naval Air Station at Yeovilton, Somerset.

1937 MILES M. 14 A MAGISTER   Acquired 1970

Span: 33ft. 10ins.
Empty weight: 1286 lbs.
Power: 130 hp DH Gipsy Major I 4-cylinder inverted inline

The Miles Magister, as the first monoplane trainer to be ordered for service with the Royal Air Force, owed its existence to the series of civil Hawks designed by F.G. Miles, the first of which, the M.2, flew from Woodley, near Reading in March 1933.

Because a supply of Cirrus engines had been obtained at give-away prices from a company that had gone into liquidation, the Hawk was able to penetrate the private-owner market very effectively at an ex-factory price of only £395! The design was developed, not surprisingly to become powered by the ubiquitous de Havilland Gipsy Major, and the first M2F Hawk Major (temporarily cleaned-up as a single-seater) gained 2nd place in the King's Cup Air Race of 1934 at 147 mph. From then on, the long line of Miles low-wing monoplanes developed at a fast pace. These included the special racing Hawk Speed-Six, three of which were built and the only surviving specimen of which, G-ADGP, is on long loan to the Shuttleworth Collection.

Before the all-wood M.14A Magister entered service, to specification T40/36, a Hawk Major had been delivered to the RAF in 1936 and 13 Hawk Trainers (progressively modified Majors) were used by the new Elementary and Reserve Flying School at Woodley. The more robust 'Maggie', though, joined the Service in September 1937 with the delivery of L 5913 to the Central Flying School. Subsequently 1242 were built for the RAF and these served with no fewer than 16 Elementary Flying Training Schools. Unlike the Tiger Moth, which continued in

military use for a further six years, the Magister was declared obsolete at the end of the war, although the author remembers one lone camouflaged specimen stored among the Tigers at No. 3 EFTS, Shellingford, in May 1947.

The idea behind the Magister was to provide a trainer with a configuration closely related to the many operational monoplanes that were entering the RAF in the late thirties. A low wing setting, vacuum-operated split trailing edge flaps, a meaningful stall and a requirement for very positive action to effect spin recovery (later softened slightly with the introduction of fuselage strakes) provided the Service with an elementary trainer geared to the needs of the time. Although in the early stages some pupils reverted to the biplane for advanced tuition on the Hart or Hind trainer, the majority progressed to more powerful monoplanes such as the Miles Master or, later, the North American Harvard. Many who were destined to fly twin-engined aircraft moved on to the Airspeed Oxford. From the aspect of acquiring handling skills, there could be no better training combinations.

After the war, no fewer than 148 Magisters were released from RAF use and became registered under the civil name of Hawk Trainer III. The type achieved success in the air racing field, cleaned-up in a number of ways, including neat conversions to single-seaters and taping the gaps between the wings and ailerons. Several were used by flying clubs for training private pilots and ATC cadets on an Air Ministry contract basis, perhaps the most numerous being the light and dark blue machines operated by Air Schools Ltd at Wolverhampon, Derby and Elstree. When in 1956 the Air Registration Board (predecessors of today's Airworthiness Division of the Civil Aviation Authority) mistrusted aircraft with wooden box spars, most Magisters were scrapped, but a handful remained in private ownership for a few years. So, in effect, a good aeroplane died prematurely.

The Exhibit: P 6382. One of only 3 preserved airworthy Magisters in the world. Often incorrectly quoted as being G-AJDR, as the aircraft arrived at Old Warden wearing that registration. However, logbook inspection revealed an earlier change of fuselage (to which an aeroplane's identity is attached) to that of P 6352, which had not held a civil registration. Restored to fly by Shuttleworth apprentices, building-in components from three specimens.

1941 SUPERMARINE SPITFIRE Vc   Acquired 1961

Span: 32ft. 2ins.
Empty weight: 5200 lbs.
Power: 1440 hp Rolls-Royce Merlin 45 or 46 12-cylinder liquid-cooled Vee.

Perhaps no aircraft is as well known to so many people as is the Spitfire. For many years almost a legend, the true Supermarine Spitfire first saw daylight under its wheels on 5th March 1936, although the type owed much to the earlier S.6 seaplanes of Schneider Trophy fame. Before the familiar elliptical wing of the Spitfire appeared, however, a single-seat fighter designated the Supermarine F7/30 had flown, with an inverted gull (cranked) wing, a fixed undercarriage, an open cockpit and powered by the steam-cooled Rolls-Royce Goshawk engine. Strangely, this fulfilled the requirements of the original Air Ministry specification, but its famous designer, the late R.J. Mitchell, was at work on something better on a private venture basis.

So the Spitfire was born. Conforming to a revised A.M. requirement F37/34, this incorporated the new 1030 hp Merlin engine and (apart from a few very early examples) eight instead of four machine guns in the wings. Within three months of the prototype's first flight, an initial order was placed for 310 aircraft, but production difficulties delayed deliveries and the first batch was five months late in reaching Service units. However, such was the Spitfire's success that shortly after the start of World War II orders totalled 4000 aircraft.

The first Spitfires were delivered to No. 19 Squadron at Duxford, arriving in July 1938, eight months later than the first Hawker Hurricanes joined No. 111 Squadron at Northolt; in each case these new aircraft were replacements for ageing Gloster Gauntlets, which were the Gladiator's immediate predecessor. The early Spitfires had two-blade fixed-pitch propellers and relatively poor take-off performance, but the type was ripe for development, with three-blade variable pitch propellers and domed cockpit canopies becoming standard equipment while the aircraft was still at the Mark I stage.

By the outbreak of war nine RAF Squadrons were equipped with Spitfires, with eighteen squadrons using Hurricanes. The two types shared the brunt of the Battle of Britain between them, with the Spitfire's superior speed and the Hurricane's manoeuvrability used to maximum advantage.

Development and mark numbers followed in rapid succession. From August 1940, IIbs exchanged the mark I's standard eight-gun layout for four .303 machine guns and two 20 mm cannon. Although best known for its activities as a fighter, early in the Spitfire's career it was adapted for high-speed high-level photographic reconnaissance, stripped of all armament, with production of the PR IV amounting to 230 aircraft.

Some marks were more notable than others and, without doubt, the V was a winner. With the Merlin 45 developing 410 hp more than the early variant, both the performance and the extent of the aircraft's use were increased. Mark Vs were the first to be used as fighter bombers, taking part in offensive sweeps across Europe, and were the first to be used extensively overseas. Many operated with clipped wings for increased performance and roll-rate at low level. The V was followed by the IX and these two variants became the most widely used of all marks.

Throughout the Spitfire's operational life, development continued. Some were fitted with extended wings of 40ft. span to improve high-altitude performance to combat high-flying German raiders, the rear top fuselage was lowered to provide improved all-round view from a bubble canopy, the rudder was

extended upwards to a pointed tip and a four-bladed propeller was introduced. After the XVI, however, the type underwent some of its most drastic modifications, exchanging the Merlin for the Griffon and offering a marked change in appearance with a longer nose and larger-chord rudder. One of the most impressive performers among the late-mark Spitfires was the PR 19, which outclassed the early jet fighters at altitude; it was this variant that carried out the last operational sortie by any front-line Spitfire, with a reconnaissance by a machine of No. 81 Squadron over Malaya on 1st April 1954.

At one time in the late fifties, only a single Spitfire (Mark Vc AB 510/G-AISU, owned by its makers) was flying, but progressively the number has increased. The Royal Air Force Battle of Britain Flight at Coningsby in Lincolnshire operates a mark II, a Vb and two 19s, while privately-owned machies include a I, a rare two-seat Mark T VIII and a pair of IXs, with one of two airworthy Griffon-powered XIVs owned by Rolls-Royce and based at East Midlands Airport.

The Exhibit: Mark Vc AR501/G-ASII. Built by Westland Aircraft at Yeovil, Somerset and issued to No. 310 (Czech) Squadron at Duxford in 1942. Later on the strength of the RAF's Central Gunnery School. Used post-war as an instructional airframe at Loughborough College, before transfer to the Collection and restoration to flying condition for use in the film 'The Battle of Britain'. Stored for several years at Old Warden; later restoration to a very high standard was completed by a volunteer crew at Duxford, with which it is operated on a joint basis. The only Spitfire flying with clipped wings, or with an original three-blade propeller.

(Another Spitfire — a PRXI — is owned by the Collection but is not on public view; see Appendix I).

1946 DHC-I CHIPMUNK   Acquired 1969

Span: 34ft. 4ins.
Empty weight: 1417 lbs.
Power: 145 hp DH Gipsy Major 8 (10/2 in civil use) 4-cylinder inverted inline.

The Chipmunk was a logical development in the long line of de Havilland light aeroplanes, although it was unusual in two ways: firstly, wooden construction had given way to an all-metal structure and, secondly, it was designed and originally produced in Canada, which accounts for the DHC designation.

The prototype Chipmunk, CF-DIO-X, flew for the first time at Toronto on 22nd May 1946 and 218 were built in Canada, with a gap of more than five years between the two main production batches; the last 60 for the Royal Canadian Air Force emerged as late as 1956. In Britain, production started in 1949 to Air Ministry specification 8/48, with first deliveries to Oxford University Air Squadron at Kidlington (now Oxford Airport) in February 1950. Subsequently the type equipped all 17 UASs, the Reserve Flying Schools, the Primary Flying Squadron and, later, the Air Experience Flights that provide flying for ATC and CCF cadets.

The Chipmunk was relatively expensive as a new aeroplane, so home civil sales from the factory were restricted to a pair for the Ministry of Transport and Civil Aviation and six for Air Service Training at Hamble. However, the RAF Reserve schools closed in 1953 and after a period in storage at Maintenance Units, large numbers were sold. They were nearly-new aircraft and inexpensive to buy, so they appealed to several flying schools and clubs, but the airworthiness authority of the time deemed the

Service version, the T.10, to fall short of civil requirements and called for extensive and expensive modifications. The result was a civil variant designated the T.22. The largest numbers of these were operated by the Airways Aero Club (replacing Auster Aiglets) and by Air Schools Ltd., the latter's light and dark blue machines replacing ageing Magisters (Hawk Trainer IIIs) in 1956-57.

The Chipmunk was one of the most pleasant light aeroplanes to handle, with well harmonised controls that were more akin to those of a heavier machine. However, as with most trainers, it suffered from spin recovery problems; these resulted first in the fitting of broad-chord rudders, which achieved little result, followed several years later by fuselage strakes.

The DHC-1 is a far more significant aeroplane than most people appear to appreciate. It has outstripped both the legendary Avro 504 and the Tiger Moth in terms of length of military service, with the unique distinction that after more than 30 years with the RAF, it is the only type that serves in the eighties with all three British Services: in the Royal Air Force with the Air Experience Flights and, in 1979 reintroduced as the primary trainer; at Middle Wallop where all army pilots receive their basic tuition on the type: and with the Britannia Flight at Plymouth to give air experience to cadets from the Royal Naval College at Dartmouth. Roughly comparable numbers are in civil use with groups and private owners.

The Exhibit: WB 588/G-AOTD: Constructor's No. 0040. Built 1950. An early release from the RAF following closure of the Reserve Schools. Stored at RAE Farnborough and later Bedford before being given to the Collection. Stored again for 10 years until restoration was undertaken by a volunteer group from British Aerospace, Kingston.

1950 PERCIVAL P. 56 PROVOST   Acquired 1969

Span: 35ft. 2ins.
Empty weight: 3350 lbs.
Power: 550 hp Alvis Leonides 9-cylinder radial.

The Percival Provost ended an era, in that it was the last piston-engined basic trainer to be delivered to the Royal Air Force, initially powered by an Armstrong-Siddeley Cheetah. Following trials in competition with the Handley Page HPR2, the Provost won the production contract to specification T. 16/48, standardising on the Leonides engine for all but the first two prototypes.

The Provost replaced the Prentice in RAF Flying Training Schools; and a far more popular aircraft it was with all concerned, with an impressive climb and speed performance and exceptional manoeuvrability. Unfortunately the available power output was reduced by gating the throttle after several Leonides engines had blown their cylinder heads, but even with restricted boost the result was very impressive for a trainer.

A student trained on the Prentice progressed from this to the Harvard at the same flying school on what was known as the "all-through" scheme, but with the Provost's entry into service, the basic and advanced stages were separated and the second phase of a pilot's course was carried out at another unit in the jet-powered Vampire T.11. Provosts formed the equipment of FTSs at South Cerney, Ternhill, Hullavington (later Syerston), Feltwell and Worksop, while at the RAF College, Cranwell, they replaced Chipmunks rather than Prentices.

With the development of a mainly jet air force, a logical move was to introduce a similarly powered basic trainer. Hunting

Percival Aircraft of Luton put forward plans for a machine that would incorporate many piston-Provost parts and in March 1953 an order was placed for nine pre-production jet Provosts for evaluation purposes. These early aircraft were used at Hullavington where courses of students were trained alongside each other on the piston and jet variants.

Clearly the results were successful, for in 1957 an order was placed for an improved version, the jet Provost T.3, which from 1959 progressively became the standard training type. In the eighties, later variants of the same aircraft remain in this role.

By 1961 the piston Provost had ended its career as a basic trainer for the Royal Air Force, but small numbers were retained for use at the Central Air Traffic Control School at Shawbury, the last Service specimen retiring late in 1969. However, the type remained in use for several years with the Irish Air Corps and the Rhodesian Air Force, the latter flying Provosts with rockets for low-level operational duties.

An early jet Provost I, registered as a civil aeroplane as G-AOBU, for use as a sales demonstrator and later for trials with the Viper engine, is owned by the Shuttleworth Collection and is on loan to Loughborough University as an instructional airframe.

The Exhibit: XF 836. Acquired from the RAF in 1969. Served with the RAF College, Cranwell and the Central Air Traffic Control School, Shawbury. Painted in Cranwell colours for the Collection by RAF St. Athan in 1977.

Chapter 6
Aero Engines
by Jocelyn Millard

Jocelyn Millard was with the de Havilland Aircraft Co. in the thirties and again after World War II during which he flew as a Hurricane pilot in the Battle of Britain. Today he is Information Officer for the Shuttleworth Collection, after 20 years with the Quality Assurance Directorate of the Ministry of Defence. He is responsible for guided tours, the library and education services.

The first accounts of man's attempt to fly are legendary, but it is certain that from the earliest times he tried to imitate the bird with its graceful flight and easy motion through the air.

The ability of birds to fly, and the consequent desire to master the air, have, through all ages spurred man on to steady and untiring efforts to become their equal. Once the barriers of flight had been overcome, there then followed for man endless dreams of methods of propulsion, and inevitably, the necessary power to create the propelling force for all the machines he was to make and fly.

In 1250, and long before any conquest of the air, Roger Bacon, English monk, alchemist and author, in his "Secrets of Art and Nature" referred to the moving of artificial wings to beat the air in the manner of a bird, and thus to him can probably be attributed the earliest reasoned speculations relating to propulsion in the air. The idea of sustentation and propulsion in the air by means of artificially flapped wings was inherent in all the early proposals for the accomplishment of mechanical flight. Leonardo da Vinci gave some considerable scientific thought to such possibilities and subsequently designed and built several flying machines on this principle. However, they are more of historic interest than practical value.

Over the period of the years of early air conquest all manners of propulsion were devised, from the use of manually activated oars in balloons to paddles, sails, and propellers. Even the possibility of propulsion resulting from the emission of a jet of air or steam was considered, and many other methods about which much could be written.

Behind all these ideas was always the one common pursuit; the prime mover for use in any kind of airborne craft, a problem which occupied the minds of all those who speculated seriously in regard to flight by man.

Sir George Cayley (1774-1875) a great pioneer of mechanical flight, gave deep thought to this question, being convinced that the development of a suitable engine was a prerequisite for progress. In his early proposals he favoured craft propelled by steam, but in his later writings he seemed to show a preference for the crude form of internal combustion engine utilizing gas, which at that time was being used experimentally. The disadvantages of the steam engine for aircraft propulsion, entailing as it did, considerable weight, and danger from fire, were fully realized, but in the absence of any other prime mover being sufficiently developed to render its application feasible, steam was the only power available. Many notable personalities were associated with the development and application of steam power in aircraft; William Samuel Henson, Horatio Phillips, Clement Ader, Sir Hiram Maxim, Henri Giffard and John Stringfellow to name but a few, and their achievements and successes in this field are too many to record.

Plate I   Le Rhone 80 hp 9 cylinder Rotary Radial Engine

The engine is the very heart of the flying machine, but the flying machine unlike most machines requires a light heart, and it was the heavy heart, the heavy engine of the past which created one of the major obstacles to successful flying. The low power-to-weight ratio of the steam engine was undoubtedly one of the undesirable aspects which urged inventors and designers to pursue the task of being able to produce a unit in which the power-to-weight ratio would not be too detracting from the performance of the flying machine.

Before turning to the advent of the internal combustion engine it is of interest to note that whilst steam was playing a very prominent part in the propulsion of both heavier and lighter-than-air craft, there were in 1883-1884 two instances in which electrical power had been used for the propulsion of aircraft. The first was a dirigible constructed by two brothers, Albert and Gaston Tissandier, and which was fitted with a Siemens electric motor of nominally 1.5 hp weighing 121 lbs. The current to drive the motor was supplied by four bichromate batteries weighing approximately 500 lbs, and the motor power was absorbed by a light two bladed airscrew measuring 9 ft in diameter. After preliminary tests the dirigible succeded in flying for two hours, and although it was not able to fly directly against the wind it was able to execute turns to the right and to the left.

Following the construction of this dirigible, another and more successful one was designed and constructed by Commandant Renard, Director of the Military Establishment at Chalais-Meudon near Paris, in collaboration with other officers. It was fitted with a Gramme electric motor developing 9 hp, the current being supplied from chromium chloride cells. The power from the motor was transmitted through a hollow shaft to an airscrew positioned at the front of the craft. On its first ascent the dirigible was manoeuvred with ease under its own power and eventually returned to the starting point.

Many subsequent ascents were made and proved to be even more successful than the first. Successful as the ventures were, the objection to the continued use of electrical power for propulsion was the weight of the storage batteries which had to be carried. The drawbacks, inseparable from the use of electric power for propulsion in the air, led to the eventual abandonment of further development along these lines.

Towards the latter half of the nineteenth century various people were seeking to produce an engine which would result in a

Plate II   Rolls-Royce Falcon 260 hp in line vee 12 cylinder

high power-to-weight ratio without having the encumbrances associated with steam engines, and in Germany in 1872, Paul Haenlein made a very early application of a primitive internal combustion engine. He attained a speed of about 10 m.p.h. in a balloon propelled by an engine of the type designed by Lenoir which used gas as a fuel, and which, in this case, was drawn from the balloon itself.

The engine developed approximately 6 hp. Experiments along these lines could not be prolonged because the buoyancy of the balloon was decreased with the continued use of the carrying gas. The need to use the carrying gas was in itself a disadvantage, and the alternatives which necessitated having a gas producing plant, or even a storage container, also constituted drawbacks with their resultant increase in weight.

In 1876 Dr. N.A. Otto successfully developed an internal combustion engine of the four stroke type using liquid fuel, and his principle of four strokes to a complete cycle, commonly known as the Otto Cycle needs no introduction nor explanation. The principle was adopted by Daimler with the intention of

111

evolving a satisfactory engine for the motor car, and his concentration on the perfection of a small high speed petrol engine had an unseen bearing on the future of mechanical flight. It will suffice to say that within the space of a few years, the weight of this type of engine had been reduced from about 100 lbs per hp to less than one tenth of that weight. The first application, for aerial propulsion, of an internal combustion engine using liquid fuel was made by Baumgarten and Wolfert in 1879 when they used a Daimler engine for the propulsion of a dirigible balloon.

By this time the field of engine development was rapidly broadening, and whilst the engines which were being designed followed the then accepted style of having vertical cylinders, Charles Manly, an assistant to Professor Samuel Pierpoint Langley defied the ethics of convention. In 1903 he produced a five cylinder watercooled engine of radial configuration. It developed 50 hp and weighed only 187.4 lbs complete with all the accessories etc. radiator, tanks, ignition system; or 3.75 lbs per hp. This remarkable achievement indicated beyond doubt that

Plate III   Bristol Cherub 34 hp Horizontally Opposed 2 cylinder

there were unlimited possibilities in the design of engines for aircraft propulsion; a field of engineering which was to be exploited to the full in the years that followed.

Whilst designers were still striving to improve all aspects of aero engines they were aided by the parallel development and introduction of new materials and techniques which contributed not only towards greater efficiency but also towards greater reliability.

From about 1909 up to the beginning of the World War I period there were aero engine designers and manufacturers in many parts of the world, and whose names are still renowned today. Between them they produced a wide range of designs in both mechanical innovations and configurations, such as the vertical type, vee and the horizontally opposed, and radial, both rotary and static; the latter having Fan and Y types of cylinder arrangements.

Nearly all these engines worked on the four stroke principle although there were a few two strokes. The number of cylinders ranged from two to twelve, and were either watercooled or aircooled. In all, about fifty different types were made in the period, many of which went into production. Many of these engines exist today, and the Shuttleworth Collection is fortunate in having several which are still flying; the Le Rhone 9 cylinder 110 hp, Le Rhone 9 cylinder 80 hp, Gnome 7 cylinder 50 hp, Anzani 3 cylinder Fan type 25 hp, and the Anzani 3 cylinder Y type 35 hp, to name but a few.

Whilst making reference to the working engines at the Shuttleworth Collection it would be appropriate here to mention in particular the Rolls-Royce Falcon and the Benz engines, both of which are also still flying, but are of the post 1914 period.

The brief account of the 1909-1914 engine development period would not be complete without reference to a man who was responsible for the first real step forward in engine design in England. He was H.P. Green. He produced a vertical engine which developed 40 brake horse power and weighed only 188 lbs, or 4.7 lbs per horse power, which was quite a considerable improvement over the power-to-weight ratio of the Wright Brothers engine.

His follow-up was another vertical engine but with six cylinders developing 120 hp and weighing 440 lbs, or only 3.66 lbs per hp, again another notable advance in the aim for improvements on the power to weight ratio. Many of his 35 hp

Plate IV   Bristol Jupiter 400 hp static radial engine, 9 cylinder

engines were used in the first Avro biplanes and later in the well-known Roe IV Triplane. His design successes were many, and in 1914 he won the prize of £5000 offered for the best aero engine in the Naval and Military Aeroplane Engine Competition.

The advent of war in 1914 immediately emphasised the importance of factors other than that of weight reduction. The aeroplane had become a major weapon of war, and the roles it was being called upon to carry out necessitated advancements in both airframe and engine. The increased range required, greater reliability, and ease of maintenance to minimise aircraft losses due to engine failure, better accessibility, and where rapidity of manoeuvre was essential, a shorter engine with more power and instant response to control, were the tasks now facing the designers.

Following the need for improvement in aero engines, some indication of the progress made in weight reduction can be seen in the table given below:—

Cooling	1914	1915	1916	1917	1918	1919	Approx weight in lbs. per hp of engine without accessories
Water	4.05	3.75	3.40	2.80	2.60	2.20	
Air	4.00	3.00	2.60	2.10	2.00	1.90	

114

With the cessation of hostilities in 1918 there occured a lull in the production of aircraft engines in all the leading countries owing to the small demand for engines for commercial use. In the after years it was found that the ultra light air cooled radial engine was not sufficiently robust for commercial use, and after a period of experimental development there emerged the advanced series of the now famous Napier Lion engines which, with the already well-established Rolls-Royce Eagle engine, the Siddeley Puma, and the Liberty engines, together with many other well-known engines, provided the power units for larger aircraft.

The progress in design and development of aero engines had now reached the stage where the knowledge and experience gained from the past provided the background and basis for future engines of outstanding reliability and performance. Designers had for some time realised that one of the answers to more power was not bigger cylinders but more of them. The famous range of Bristol engines with their double banks of cylinders, and the 24 cylinder H type Napier Dagger engine are supreme examples of successful designs based on that theory.

It is beyond the capacity of a preface to give a comprehensive

Plate V   The Gipsy Major 10 MK. 2

account of all the aspects of engine design which have evolved and been developed over the many years, and perhaps they are best summarised by saying that engine performance and reliability were greatly increased as a result of remarkable advancements in fuel and ignition systems, lubrication methods and systems, fuel and oil technology and hydraulics, in addition to many mechanical developments. The use of superchargers, the introduction of the sleeve valve, and the continued use of the reduction gear all played major parts in the improvement of efficiency and performance.

Following the birth of the Cirrus engines used in the renowned Moth and other aircraft, there came the world famous Gipsy engines, unsurpassed at anytime in reliability and popularity. They were used in the inverted position, a design innovation introduced to give the pilot a better view and the aircraft cleaner lines.

In parallel with the production of the de Havilland range of engines, Rolls-Royce produced their line of Kestrel and Merlin engines, as also did the Bristol Company with their equally famous range of radial engines named after the Gods in Greek mythology.

All these engines were produced in a succession of "Series", each "Series" indicating that a change or improvement had been embodied, and all towards one end; the maximum possible efficiency and reliability.

The factors relating to efficiency and reliability have so far centred around improvements in design aspects, and no mention has been made of the propeller and the important part it plays in the propulsion of airborne craft. No synopsis of aero engines would be complete without a reference to a device which has been and still is the major item without which the internal combustion aero engine cannot function.

The idea of using a propeller as a means of propulsion began in the era of Leonardo da Vinci, when he conceived the notion of a lifting screw or helicopter. Crude in form, it was nonetheless an invention of some significance. In 1784 a French Officer, General Jean Baptiste Marie Meusnier suggested the use of the screw as an air propeller for propulsion in a forward plane and this idea was to pave the way for the development of the airscrew for many years to follow, and well into the twentieth century. Once the airscrew had become the accepted means of propulsion, engine designers and manufacturers were rapidly realizing that the

Plate VI   Rolls-Royce Avon turbo jet, axial flow compressor

theory involved in propeller design was intricate and extensive.

Progress of time produced progress in design, as propellers of almost countless shapes and sizes appeared in which were attempts to embody all the known factors essential for maximum efficiency; such as diameter, pitch, blade width, pitch ratio, peripheral speed, and not least of all, consideration of propeller slip.

The propeller which is the most efficient is the one which will produce the greatest amount of thrust in proportion to the power transmitted to it by the engine, both whilst revolving on the ground and when travelling through the air. A propeller which is too large or of too great a pitch for a given engine will prevent the latter from developing its normal power by retarding its speed. Propeller blades which are of insufficient area or pitch will allow the engine to race due to inadequate loading, and if the speed is allowed to become too great, the blades if made of wood, could disintegrate on reaching their critical rotational limits. No doubt with this possibility in mind, the designers provided for the strongest construction that available materials and manufacturing techniques would permit.

In the early 1930's the inevitable consequence of the search for new ideas to obtain maximum efficiency from propellers was the appearance of blades which had a two position variable pitch, fine and coarse. The Ratier propellers as fitted to the DH 88 Comet were of this type, and probably the first of their kind. They were operated centrifugally during take off, and once the coarse position had been reached, the blades could not be reset to the fine position again whilst the aircraft was airborne. The other type of this variable pitch propeller as fitted to the Fairey Battle was manually operated and could be altered whilst the engine was running, from fine position to coarse and back to fine at will at any time in the air or on the ground.

The advent of the variable pitch propeller was the opening to further innovations in this field and there finally emerged the propeller with blades which could be varied in pitch hydraulically throughout their range of movement from the fully fine to the fully coarse position. Further development produced blades which could be altered in pitch to a position where the leading edges were in line with the direction of flight; the feathered

Plate VII   Whittle Jet W2/700, centrifugal compressor

position. From this advancement, there then followed the reversible pitch position; a very useful asset in cases of emergency — in the right place and at the right time!!

As in the case of aero engine design, the design and development of propellers were accompanied by the development of new materials and techniques in all the associated branches of engineering manufacture and inspection.

The outcome of continued research and development was a wide range of propellers with blades of wood or metal, some of the latter even being hollow for lightness without loss of strength and safety, all differing in shapes from the tips to the root ends. The number of blades varied from two to six, the required number, diameter and shape being determined by the operating requirements of both engine and propeller.

The aero engines and propellers in the Shuttleworth Collection, some of which form part of the static display, whilst others still take part in annual flying events, are a good representation of those produced between the pre World War I and the post Word War II periods.

General details of the Collection's working and static engines are given in the table in the pages that follow.

SHUTTLEWORTH AERO ENGINES
IN PERIOD AND ALPHABETICAL ORDER

ILLUSTRATIONS OF SOME OF THE TYPES LISTED BELOW ARE SHOWN IN PLATES I - VII

Period	Engine	Configuration	No. of Cylinders	HP	Weight in lbs/hp	Static Display	Shuttleworth Aircraft	Type(s) used on other Aircraft	General Information
Pre 1900	Ahrbecker	Vertical	1	5	22	*		Frost Ornithopter	Steam Engine
1900 To World War I	Antoinette	Inline vee	8	30/40	2-3	*		Airship Bleriot Farman	Direct fuel injection automatic inlet valves 90° Vee
	Anzani	Static Radial Fan Type	3	25	5.6	*	Bleriot XI	Deperdussin Santos Dumont	Automatic inlet valves
	Anzani	Static Radial inverted Y type	3	35	4.03	.	Deperdussin	Bleriot Caudron	Automatic inlet valves
	Clerget	Rotary Radial Type 9Z	9	110	Approx 3	*		Avro 504K Sopwith Camel Bristol M1A	Dual Plugs Mechanically operated exhaust and inlet valves
	Gnome	Rotary Radial	7	50	Approx 3.44		Blackburn Monoplane 1912	Bleriot Deperdussin Morane	Automatic inlet valves in piston head
	J.A.P.	Inline vee	8	30		*		City of Cardiff Airship	External camshaft at bottom of Vee
	Le Rhone Plate I	Rotary Radial	9	80	Approx 3	*	Sopwith Pup	Sopwith Scout Morane Bleriot	Inlet and exhaust valves operated by one Rod. No big ends radial shoes
	Le Rhone	Rotary Radial	9	110	Approx 3		Avro 504K	Sopwith Camel Nieuport; 17CI DH5	Cam ring and transfer manifolds at rear of engine. No big ends. radial shoes

Era	Engine	Configuration	Cylinders	hp	Compression ratio	*	Aircraft	Aircraft	Notes
	Phillips	Rotary Radial	7	10-12	2.7	*		Phillips Matchless Machine	2 stroke aircooled One cylinder missing
World War I	Beardmore	Inline	6	120	5.25	*		AWFK 8 Martinsyde G100, G102	Offset cylinders Double thrust race for Tractor or pusher. Tappet rod for inlet and exhaust valves
	Benz	Inline	6	230	3.7		LVG CVI	Junkers JI Gotha CII	Separate cylinders Two exhausts per cylinder Two carburettors each supply 3 cylinders
	Napier Lion	Inline Arrow Head	12	450	2.15	*		DH 9 HP W10 HP Hendon	3 banks of 4 cylinders 60° between banks
	Rolls-Royce Falcon Plate II	Inline vee	12	260	2.7		Bristol Fighter F2b	Martinsyde FI AW. FK12 DH4	Scaled down version of Eagle. Oldest RR engine in world still flying.
	Hawk	Inline	6	100	5.9	*		Mostly Non-Rigid Airships Avro 504 F	Cylinders - wrought steel
	Wolseley Viper	Inline vee	8	180	2.7		SE5A	Avro 504K Experimental	Replaced Hispano Suiza engine
Post World War I	ABC	Horizontally Opposed	2	3	3.5		English Electric Wren		OHV Engine. Motorcycle type engine converted
	ABC Scorpion II	Horizontally opposed	2	34	3.1		DH 53	Comper Swift ABC Robin Woodpigeon	Induction manifold Integral with bottom of crankcase body
	Airdisco	Inline vee	8	120	3.5		DH 51	Parnall Gyroplane Avro 504	Designed from the 80 hp Renault by the Air Disposals Company

Period	Engine	Configuration	No. of Cylinders	HP	Weight in lbs/hp	Static Display	Shuttleworth Aircraft	Type(s) used on other Aircraft	General Information
To	Alvis Leonides	Static Radial	9	550	1.5		Hunting Percival Provost	Hunting Percival Prince / Bristol 192 Helicopter	Centrifugal impeller type supercharger supplying atomised mixture from automatic low pressure fuel injector
Pre World War II	**Armstrong Siddeley** Cheetah 15/17	Static Radial 7		420	2.1		Avro Anson C19	Single stage	Supercharger
	Genet Major	Static Radial	7	140	2.4		Cierva Autogiro C30A	Avro Cadet / Auro Avian	Modified for Avro Giro installation
	Lynx	Static Radial	7	175	2.8		Avro Tutor	Avro 504N / DH Hawk Moth	Parts are interchangeable with Jaguar and Mongoose engines
	Mongoose	Static Radial	5	125	2.8		Hawker Tomtit	Avro 504N / HP Gugnunc / Fokker S4	Parts interchangeable with Lynx and Jaguar
	Blackburne Thrush	Static Radial Inverted "Y"	3	35	3.77	*		Avro Avis / Parnall Pixie III	Specially derived for 1926 light aeroplane competition.
	Tomtit	Static Radial Inverted Vee	2	26	1.9	*		DH 53 / ANEC 1.1A	First type to fly inverted in U.K.
	Bristol Cherub Plate III	Horizontally opposed	2	34	3.0	*	Granger Archaeopteryx	Bristol Brownie / Short Satellite / Parnall Pixie	Valves radial to cylinder head

Engine	Type	Cyl.	hp	Comp. ratio		Aircraft	Aircraft	Remarks
Jupiter Plate IV	Static Radial	9	400	2	*		Very extensive	Many Mks. Four valves per cylinder. Dornier DoX flying boat fitted with twelve Jupiter engines
Mercury	Static radial	9	720	1.4		Gloster Gladiator	Bristol Bleinheim and Bolingbroke Westland Lysander	Mercury engines belonged to high altitude class, one of three classes designed to meet demands
Cirrus (ADC)	Inline	4	60/65	4.48		Avro Triplane	Miles Hawk	
Cirrus Hermes II (Blackburn)	Inline	4	105	2.9		DH 60 Moth Parnall Elf	Percival Gull Avro Avian Desoutter	Cylinder retaining bolts pass through fins
de Havilland								
Gipsy	Inline	4	85	3.35		DH 60G Gipsy Moth	Avro Avian	
Gipsy Minor	Inline inverted	4	80	2.6		DH Moth Minor		
Gipsy Major Plate V	Inline inverted	4	130	1.9		DH Moth range Miles Magister	Miles Falcon and Monarch BA Eagle	Used also in DH experimental aircraft TK 2 and TK 4
Gipsy Six	Inline inverted	6	185 STD 230 (R)	2.8 2.1	*		DH86 Percival Vega Gull Miles Hawk Speed Six	R(Racing version) originally fitted to DH 88 Comet
Gipsy Queen II	Inline inverted	6	200/210	2.58	*	DH 88 Comet	Percival Proctor	The Two Gipsy Queens to be fitted to the Comet have been overhauled especially for the project
Gipsy King	Inline inverted vee	12	505/525 Take off	2.05	*		DH 91 DH 93	Only 50 engines made

Period	Engine	Configuration	No. of Cylinders	HP	Weight in lbs/hp	Static Display	Shuttleworth Aircraft	Type(s) used on other Aircraft	General Information
	Pobjoy Niagart	Static radial	7	85	1.8		BA Swallow	Comper Kite and Swift	Double helical
	R	Static radial	7	75	2.9	*		Cierva C25 Autogiro Comper Swift	Reduction gear
	Rolls-Royce Kestrel V	Inline vee	12	640	1.34		Hawker Hind		Supercharged engine
	Kestrel XVI	Inline vee	12	745	1.30	*		Hawker Fury Hawker Hart	
	Scott Squirrel	Inline inverted	2	16 normal	5.30		Flying Flea		Motor cycle engine modified for use in light aircraft
World War II	**Rolls-Royce** Merlin 23	Inline vee	12	1280	0.94	*		Hawker Hurricane	2 piece cylinder block
	Merlin 45	Inline vee	12	1470	0.94		Supermarine Spitfire Vc		Aircraft served in 310, 312 and 422 Sqns. Used in making film 'Battle of Britain'
Post World War II	**Blackburn** Cirrus Bombardier	Inline inverted	4	180	2.11		Auster AOP 9	Skeeter Mks 3-4	Dual spark plugs vertical drive camshafts
	Cirrus Minor Inline 2A	inverted	4	100	Approx 2.25	*		Auster Autocrat Miles Gemini	

Rolls-Royce

	Type				Aircraft	Notes
Continental	Horizontally opposed flat four	4	100	2.82	Bristol Boxkite / Cierva Grasshopper Fairtravel Linnet	This type of engine can be used as a pusher or tractor
Griffon MK58	Inline vee	12	2450	0.89 *	Avro Shackleton	2 speed single stage supercharger

Gas Turbine Engines

Name or Designation	Manufacturer	Compressor	Compressor Stages	Turbine	Aircraft Types	General Information
Avon Plate VI	Rolls-Royce	Axial Flow	12	2 Stage	Caravelle, Canberra, Fairey Delta	Turbo-jet Fairey Delta raised World Speed Record to 1000 mph plus for first time
Eland	Napier	Axial Flow	10	3 stage	Fairey Rotodyne two engines	Propeller Turbine
Ghost	de Havilland	Centrifugal	1	Single stage	Comet 1 de Havilland Venom & Vixen	First jet engine in the world to obtain approval for civil transport operation
Mamba	Armstrong Siddeley	Axial flow	3	2 stage	Boulton Paul Balliol Fairey Gannet Short Seamew	Drives a propeller through a reduction gear
M 45H Mk 501	Rolls-Royce	Axial flow	5 low P 7 high P	Single stage HP Turbine 3 stage low P	VFW 614	Generally known as a twin spool medium by-pass turbo-fan
Viper Mk 601-22	Rolls-Royce Bristol	Axial flow	8	2 stage	HS 125 Hunting Percival Jet Provost	Made in 1972. Used by Rolls-Royce as bench development engine for Hawker Siddeley 125 Aircraft
Whittle Jet W2/700 Plate VII	Power Jets	Centrifugal	1	Single Stage	Gloster E28/39	Some flight testing carried out in a prototype Gloster Meteor E28, and in the tail of the Wellington flying test bed

Chapter 7
Other Aviation Exhibits
by Jocelyn Millard

Man-powered aircraft

Amongst the many exhibits in the Shuttleworth Collection which attract the attention of visitors of all ages are three, man-powered machines.

These aircraft all made history in their day, and with their achievements, now many years in the past, they have become non flying exhibits in secluded retirement.

Sumpa: Southampton University Man-Powered Aircraft

This aircraft was designed and built between the summer of 1960 and the summer of 1961 at the University of Southampton by postgraduate students who were assisted financially by the Royal Aeronautical Society. The aircraft made its first flight from an airfield in Hampshire in the late afternoon of the 9th November, 1961. The pilot was Mr. Derek Piggot. The aircraft became airborne after a short run when under power from the pilot, and flew for a distance of 70 yards, attaining a height of 6ft.

This brief flight made aeronautical history in England as it was the first occasion on which man had risen from the ground and flown in a controlled manner solely by means of muscle power.

At this particular time, such a feat had been perfomed only once before; on a Bossi-Bonomi man-powered aircraft in Italy in 1937.

It was the Kremer prize of £5,000 offered in 1960 for man-powered flight which stimulated the idea to construct the aircraft, but it never flew completely around the course which had been planned for the occasion.

After further development and modifications, the aircraft was extensively altered in an attempt to improve reliability and control. It subsequently crashed, severely damaging the structure, and as a consequence it was decided not to do any more flying in this machine.

The University of Southampton repaired it and loaned it to the Shuttleworth Collection for exhibition.

Jupiter

The original aircraft was designed and partly constructed by Mr. C.H. Roper of Woodford. After a serious fire the remains of the aircraft were taken to the No. 1 School of Technical Training, RAF Halton, in 1970. After some modifications to the design, the Staff and Apprentices rebuilt the machine and completed the work in the late 1971.

Jupiter's maiden flight took place at RAF Benson on 9th February 1972, and intensive flight trials in the following months led to rapid improvements in handling skills.

Although the best flight made was a distance of 1355 yards (1.24 Km) on 16th June 1972, the best officially recorded flight was only 1171 yards (1.07 Km) on June 29th in the same year. Both flights were made by Flight Lieutenant John Potter.

Jupiter's record flight was beaten in 1976 by Japan's Stork aircraft, a machine remarkably similar to Jupiter in design, but considerably lighter.

In Britain, Jupiter still retains the distance and duration records for man-powered flight.

Toucan II

The Toucan man-powered machines were designed by a group of Handley Page Aeronautical Engineers who in 1965 formed the

Hertfordshire Pedal Aeronauts, and being motivated by the Kremer prize for man-powered flight. Following design studies, with the support of the Royal Aeronautical Society, construction commenced in April 1967. The first machine to be produced was the Toucan 1. In view of the nature of the project the prime consideration was lightness combined with strength, thus it was essential that many of the materials used in the construction differed in some respects from the materials used in the construction of the ordinary light aircraft. Where metallic materials were necessary, aluminium alloy components were used, the particular alloy being accepted in the aircraft industry as one having a very satisfactory strength to weight ratio. The non metallic materials consisted of spruce, balsa wood, polystyrene, and melinex, the latter being a very thin transparent material used for covering the airframe and propeller.

Toucan 1 was completed after some 20,000 hours of labour. On the 23rd December 1972 it made its first flight and covered a distance of 68 yards. This was the world's first flight of a two seater man-powered machine, and another milestone in English aviation history had been reached.

Developments continued, and on 3rd July 1973 it made its best flight when it covered a distance of 700 yards in 1 minute 20 seconds, and reached a height of about 18 ft.

Following some serious damage, the machine was reconstructed in 1974 and the wing span was increased by 16 ft to 139 ft. The machine then became known as Toucan II. It proved to be a stable aircraft and easy controllable.

Control in the pitching or looping plane was by the tailplane which was movable, and control in the rolling and yawing plane by slot lip ailerons.

Owing to the position of the propeller, at the aft end of the machine, there is no rudder. The photograph shows Toucan II in flight.

The exhibit was presented to the Collection in October 1978.

Powered Hang Glider VJ 23

Techanical Details:
Engine: McCulloch 101, 2 stroke, 123 cc, 9 hp.
Span: 32 ft.
Length: 17 ft.
Weight: 135 lbs.
Endurance: 1¼ hours.
Range: 45 miles.
Speed Range: 15-30 mph.
Ceiling: 5000 ft.

Although this craft is generally referred to as a powered hang glider its structure and method of control render it more in keeping with a light aircraft. Unlike the original hang glider of recent times which has no control surfaces other than the wing which supports it, and which is dependent on the movement of the pilot's body for changing direction and attitude, the exhibit has conventional wings and tail plane with their respective control surfaces. There is no fuselage as such, but a light alloy tubular boom serves the same purpose for constructional

convenience, and it is this which gives the craft its aircraft-like appearance.

The one feature which discriminates it from the light aircraft is the absence of proper seating accommodation for the pilot who flies whilst seated on a small suspended platform and supported by his underarms within a framework at the front of the machine.

It is recorded as being the first powered hang glider to cross the channel, on May 9th 1978. Almost three years to the day it was presented to the Shuttleworth Collection by Duckhams on May 8th 1981.

The exhibit was built and piloted by Mr. David Cook of Aldringham, Suffolk who had achieved many notable successes in the machine.

Purely by co-incidence, Mr. Cook's birthday is the same as Bleriot's: 25th July. They both made their channel crossing at the age of 37.

Lighter-than-air Exhibits

Although the progress in design and development of aircraft and aircraft engines over the first fifty years of the twentieth century is very much in evidence in the Shuttleworth Collection, such a comparative representation of lighter-than-air craft is regrettably not possible. As it is unlikely that the Collection will ever be able to have realistic exhibits in the foreseeable, or even the unforeseeable future, it presents as an alternative, albeit an inadequate one, a collection of models, relics, photographs and printed matter in the hope that the exhibits will be of interest to all.

The special section is dominated by three exhibits, two model airships, and an airship engine. Whilst the engine may be little known to the public in general the same cannot be said for the two airships, the R 100, and the R 101. The last era of airships was one of rigid dirigibles, and it might be of interest to briefly preface their origin. In 1852, Henri Giffard, a Frenchman, made an elongated balloon and this craft opened the way to the development of airships. In the early airships a gas filled envelope was used, and from this, the power and passenger accommodation was suspended by a system of rigging. This type of craft was known as non rigid.

As power units and passenger loads became heavier, the suspended load caused the gas filled envelope to distort. This drawback was overcome by the fitting of a rigid keel to the base of the envelope to support the load and the type then became known as the semi-rigid. As loads increased it was evident that further stiffening of the structure was essential, and the result was the dirigible with an entirely rigid framework, a method of construction which was to be adopted by designers in the years that followed. Advance in airship construction was, however, hindered by expense, not only of the airship itself, but also of satisfactory hangarage. However, the obstacle of expense took second place to enthusiasm, and experiments were continued in many places.

The R 100 and R 101
In 1920, the Air Council took over from the Admiralty the control of British airships, and on their advice the government of the day gave orders for the disbandment of the Airship Service. On May 14th, 1924, after discussions which lasted for two years, the Prime Minister announced that the Government had decided to initiate a comprehensive programme of research into problems relating to airship services. The Government also decided to retain both Cardington and Pulham stations and commission them. The Air Ministry was to construct airship bases overseas and give the Airship Guarantee Company the first contract for an airship to be built for commercial purposes. This was to be the R 100. The Air Ministry also was to build an airship, and which was to be the R 101; thus was the start of an authorized programme for three years.

The main conditions which the two craft had to meet were; a volume of 5,000,000 cu.ft. giving a lift of 150 tons, strength to ensure definite safety factors, a cruising speed of 63 mph, and an attainable speed of 70 mph.

There was also to be sleeping and eating accommodation for 100 passengers. The structure weight was not to be more than 90 tons, thereby giving a useful lift of 60 tons.

The R 100 was built at Howden in Yorkshire. Designed by Barnes Wallis, an engineeer and designer who needs no introduction, it was 709 ft long and 131 ft in diameter. The power plants were six Rolls-Royce Condor engines of 700 hp each, and each driving separate propellers. The engines were mounted end to end in three cars, two being wing cars and the third on the centreline of the airship towards the aft end.

On November 11th 1929, lift and trim trials were carried out and it was found that the useful lift was some seven tons less than had been calculated. The first trial flight took place on December 16th of the same year, and the R 100 flew to Cardington with a crew of 45 and 12 passengers.

The journey took 5 hours 3 mins. There then followed many months of improvements and more and more flight trials, there were also many mishaps which necessitated making modifcations and repairs. On 29th July 1930 the R 100 left Cardington for Montreal, Canada, and arrived at St. Hubert Airport, Montreal at 4 am on August 1st after a flight of 78 hours at an average speed of 42 miles an hour. The North Atlantic from England to Canada had been flown for the first time, but not without a price, the airship having encountered very rough weather conditions and as a result sustained a considerable amount of damage.

After a short stay and further delays, the R 100 left the mooring mast at Montreal on August 13th for the return journey to England. The homeward passage was uneventful and after 57½ hours the R 100 was moored to it's mast at Cardington. Unlike the reception in Canada where it was given a tremendous welcome, it's homecoming was silent, and it came to rest unsung and without honour. Little was it realised that the historic flight from Canada was to be the last that the R 100 was to make, for the

inconceivable airship disaster was only weeks away, and any future the R 100 had was rapidly drawing to a close. After the loss of the R101, the R 100 was eventually sold, almost in ignominy, as scrap for £450.

The R 101 was built at Cardington and the process of erection occupied two years. It was not until the end of September 1929 that it's construction according to the original plans, was complete. The volume of the airship was 5,000,000 cu.ft., its length 732 ft, and diameter 132 ft.

The passenger accommodation consisted of a lounge 33 ft long and 62 ft wide with a promenade at each end from which an excellent view could be obtained. The designers were very unconventional in many of their ideas in that they extended not only to the general structure of the hull, but to important details such as gas-bag wiring, gas valves at each side of the bags instead of at the top and bottom, and the rudders operated by servo motors. The airship was powered by five Beardmore diesel oil engines each of 585 horsepower, and carried in five separate cars. Originally, reversing propellers were fitted, but they proved to be unsuccessful. The alternative was in having four of the five engines to provide the forward motion, and the fifth to move astern.

This latter engine was carried for the sole purpose of operating for only minutes at a time when the craft was landing or taking off. When installed in its car the engine weighed over three tons, something of a parasitic necessity. Like the R 100 which was found to be unable to meet it's calculated useful lift requirements, the R101 was also unable to meet the requirements and it was calculated to be about 25 tons heavy.

The first trial flight was made on October 14th 1929 which lasted $5\frac{1}{2}$ hours. Again, like the R 100, in the months that followed the first trial flight there were modifications, repairs, mishaps; too many to detail.

By now a decision to fly the R 101 to India had been made, and amongst the large number of modifications which were constantly needed, was one of major importance; how to increase the useful lift and reduce to a minimum the 25 tons of excess weight. In view of all the proposals to improve various performances, it will suffice to say that one of the most important schemes was to increase the length of the middle bay and thus provide room for an additional gas-bag, which it was hoped would add another 9 tons to the useful lift. This major change to the structure gave the airship a final length of 777 ft. The work completed, the R 101 was brought out from its hangar at 4.30 p.m on 1st October 1930, and carried out her last flight trial.

At 6.36 p.m. on the evening of October 4th the R 101 left the mooring mast at Cardington to begin her last and tragic flight. Not many hours later it crashed at Beauvais in France on route to India.

This mammoth of the skies was lost because it had been put to a test far more severe than it had ever experienced at any time in it's existence, and in that test the airship failed.

It is almost ironic that some fifty years later, the giant sheds at Cardington are again being used for another era of airships. With the advances made over the recent decades in non metallic materials, electronics, and other major requirements the Airship Industries Company has successfully built and flown a non rigid airship. Although of conventional shape it is of unique construction, the company having applied modern technology to the full to achieve success.

City of Cardiff Airship

The third of the main exhibits in the Shuttleworth lighter-than air section is the J.A.P. 30 hp vee eight engine which was used to power the airship City of Cardiff. This airship was designed by Mr. E. T. Willows and was the first aerial machine to be seen in the west of England.

Chapter 8
The Transport Exhibits

by Jocelyn Millard

Richard Shuttleworth, the founder of the Shuttleworth Collection, obtained several early road vehicles before he ventured into the field of aviation. These are described in detail in a series of booklets covering the cars, carriages, cycles, motorcycles and fire engines, so this chapter will give only a brief description of the various transport items that are held at Old Warden. Here, even more than with aeroplanes, precise dating becomes complicated, for an owner may make fairly drastic alterations to a car, even to the extent of placing a body of one year onto a chassis that is considerably older. What, then, is the correct year to quote?

Not all the road vehicles are on display all the time; through lack of exhibition space some are stored, others await technical attention and a few may be away on exhibition at other places. However, most of the items are on view and always there is a good range of cycles, horse-drawn vehicles and early cars for visitors to see. Before Richard started collecting items for preservation, some of these had been used by members of the Shuttleworth family.

Cycles:

In the cycles, we see examples of man's early attempts to propel himself unaided at something more attractive than a mere walking speed. The idea of self-propelled locomotion has existed in the minds of men for a far longer period than can be traced through existing records, so it is difficult to determine precisely when the cycle originated. It is of interest that, although there is no evidence that such a machine actually existed, the earliest reference to the subject to be found in England is a stained-glass window in a church in Stoke Poges. This window shows a rider sitting astride a crude machine which vaguely resembles the early

Hobby Horse, but it is unlikely that any connection with cycling was in the mind of the artist.

The earliest exhibit in the Collection cycle range is the Hobby Horse, and it is one of the four Boneshakers on view. The Boneshaker is the English version of the Michaux Velocipede. The Shuttleworth Hobby Horse dates from 1819. It was designed and patented by Denis Johnson, based on similar lines to that of the Draisienne or Hobby Horse designed by Charles Baron Von Drais de Sauerbrun, which was patented in 1818. The exhibit at Old Warden has wooden wheels and iron tyres. It is a ladies' version, and like the ladies' cycles of today was designed with a gap to enable the rider to mount with ease, and without embarrassment, as well as having an adjustable chest support. Propulsion is achieved by the rider sitting astride the saddle and using a striding action with the legs.

There is no provision for braking, and on a machine weighing 66 lbs such a deficiency must have deterred many a rider from venturing down any appreciable incline. Apart from occasional cleaning, the exhibit has not received any other attention. It is on long loan to the Collection by courtesy of the Science Museum.

Three other Boneshakers on view are a treadle-propelled machine of the 1865 period and two pedal machines of about 1868. Each of these three exhibits has wooden wheels with iron tyres and a braking system consisting of a twistgrip on the handlebars, interconnected with a lever which acts on the rear wheel. The treadle machine is on loan to the Collection from Mr. E. D. Fisher of Biggleswade.

Once foot-propelled machines (pedal or treadle) had become a practical proposition, variants soon made their appearance in the form of three and four-wheeled machines. Although tricycles and quadricycles had made their appearance around 1845-1846, they were somewhat crude both in design and workmanship. The tricycle exhibited in the Collection is of the 1877 period and is a great improvement on the earlier standards of workmanship. It has two large front wheels, only one of which is driven, the drive being achieved by means of crankshaft-type pedal movement.

With the drive on one wheel only, the difficulties with steering can well be imagined. At a later date the fitting of a differential helped to solve some of the problems. Steering is effected by a small trailing wheel operated by a hand grip, and a braking system is operated by a hand lever to spoon brakes acting on the solid tyres of the front wheels. Queen Victoria is reputed to have favoured this kind of tricycle.

By the 1890s there were several versions of this type, and both single-seat and two-seat versions were developed. As far as is known, no restoration work of any kind has been done on this exhibit. It is believed to have been discovered among many other relics which had been stored away in one of the Shuttleworth family buildings.

Two Pennyfarthing bicycles are exhibited and are dated as being of the 1879-1886 period. While this span of years might not be exact, it does give a good indication of the period during which the machines were in use. This type of machine is the first real departure from the Boneshaker and its successors. It is the result of improvements in materials, manufacturing methods, wheel design and experimentation in the ratios of wheel diameters.

The two exhibits are not very different from one another. One has a front wheel diameter of 56 inches and the other a front wheel diameter of 48 inches, and unless the machines were side by side a reasonable knowledge of the variants would be required to be able to distinguish one from the other. In their construction, iron and steel have taken the place of wood as used in their predecessors, and solid rubber tyres replace the iron. An interesting feature of the machine with the larger front wheel is the lamp mounted on the front spindle between the wire spokes. In the entrance to the shop at Old Warden is a photograph of Richard Shuttleworth riding one of the exhibits.

A quadricycle in the Collection was made in 1877 by James Starley, who was a bicycle pioneer of some note. It can be used either as a single-seater by removing half of the frame, or as a side-by-side tow-seater. Its basic design does not differ very greatly from the tricycle except that it has a fourth wheel at the front of the same diameter as the rear wheel. The drive is by a chain to each of the large side wheels. With four wheels there is considerable improvement in stability and control, in addition to safety. Steering is effected by a hand grip through a rack and pinion and crossed rod interconnecting each of the small wheels at the front and rear. It is believed that not many of this type of vehicle were made. The exhibit has been demonstrated in use at Old Warden on occasions.

Following on from the Penny Farthing bicycles, the Kangaroo is one of the examples of the efforts made to eliminate the many disadvantages of the former. The exhibit is dated 1884, but cycles of this type were made in the late 1870s. The Kangaroo design uses a front wheel much smaller than that of the Penny Farthing, thereby reducing the saddle height from the ground, a change which has evident advantages.

A geared-up sprocket drive to the front wheel is by a chain on each side of the wheel and from cranks placed some distance below the wheel centre. Using this method of driving enables the wheel to revolve faster than the pedals and in addition, the arrangement and location of the drive assembly allows the rider to be positioned a little farther back than is possible on the Penny Farthing, therefore making a little improvement in safety. A machine of this type won a hundred-mile race in 1885 at an average speed of 15 mph. The Shuttleworth exhibit took part in the Cavalcade of cycles at Windsor Castle on 5 June 1977.

After it became possible to gear up the drives of cycle wheels, the diameter of front and rear wheels tended to become more or less the same. A development of the bicycle along these lines resulted in a machine called the Gale Gaelic in the 1893 period. A bicycle of this type is one of the Shuttleworth exhibits and its similarity to modern designs is quite apparent.

Before leaving the cycles of the last century, one other machine is worthy of a brief note. It is the Bantam which was made by the Crypto Cycle Company of London in 1896. Structurally it differs mainly from earlier machines in that the front and rear forks are joined by two parallel horizontal members which are secured to points near the top and bottom of the front pillar, and appropriately to the rear pillar. The drive is through a Crypto epicyclic gear incorporated in the front hub which causes the pedals to rotate at a slower speed than the wheel.

Dunlop's pneumatic tyres were patented in 1888 and fitted to the Bantam cycle, which is the earliest one in the Shuttleworth range to be so fitted, although following Dunlop's patent other earlier cycles used pneumatic tyres.

One of the most interesting cycles in the range is the Ivel ladies' model of 1901. It was owned by Mrs. Shuttleworth, who rode it for many years, and well into her eighties. It was made in the nearby town of Biggleswade by Dan Albone, who was not only a racing cyclist of distinction but also a competent mechanic who had made notable contributions to the development of cycles. The Ivel got its name from the River Ivel which runs quite close to Biggleswade. Apart from the frame designed especially for ladies, the general construction is very much the same as that of the Gale Gaelic already mentioned, and again very much like the ladies' cycles of today.

There are no detailed records in the Collection which would give any indication of the extent of what was necessary to make some of the machines roadworthy, but the Peterborough Veteran Cycle Club in recent years undertook to restore the Penny Farthing, Kangaroo, Bantam and quadricycle. Their condition was such that in each case a complete rebuild was found to be necessary even to the extent of having new spindles and other items specially made.

* * *

Motor cycles:

Many motor-cycles have been loaned for exhibition on a rota basis, but several interesting specimens are owned by the Collection and these cover a wide range of ages and performance capabilities.

A machine that was well ahead of its time was the Singer of 1900 with its engine fitted within the rear wheel. This was claimed as the first engine of British design to have been used to power a bicycle in this way. It was necessary to pedal to start the motor. This early venture into the realm of powered bicycles makes an interesting comparison with the popular auto-cycles of many years later.

The same year saw the introduction of the Marot-Garden motor tricycle, powered by a $2\frac{1}{4}$ hp de Dion engine with a surface carburettor and four-volt trembler coil ignition. This could be converted to a two-seat quadricycle by replacing the front fork with a two-wheel forecar. This, too, depended on a pedal start. Only a little younger, the Aurora of 1904 with its engine of $2\frac{1}{2}$ hp is believed to be the only specimen of the kind still in existence.

Mid-way in the development of the motor-cycle and with a very popular name was the Triumph type S.D. of 1923. Its 550 cc engine drove the rear wheel by a non-slip type of belt and its performance was such that it had few serious competitors; its price was £115.

We jump now to two of the few post World War II exhibits in the Collection. The Cyclemaster, produced originally in 1950, is powered by a 32 cc two-stroke engine mounted within the rear wheel; this does not revolve, but remains stationary, transmitting its power through a clutch and cushioned drive to an internal sprocket that is similar to the one for the pedal on the outside of the wheel. The exhibit was made in 1958.

By contrast, the other post-war motor cycle is the special Vincent HRD known as 'Methamon'. In 1955 this began as a standard unsupercharged combination of 1000 cc and in this form it achieved considerable success in sprint events. Later, however, its owner decided to improve on the basic type specification by increasing the engine capacity to 1143 cc and supercharging it. The result was outstanding; the machine broke many records and in 1965 it achieved a measured 148.4 mph using methanol as fuel. This accounts for the name Methamon, which is a combination of the words methanol and monster! The combination was driven to success by its owner, Mr. Maurice Brierly of Watton-at-Stone, who kindly donated it to the Collection.

Horsedrawn Vehicles

In the story of land transport, the horse dominated the scene for many centuries until the evolution of the Iron Horse, and later the motorcar. The poor old horse also evolved. For a long time it just carried man and his package on its back — the pack horse — until it was realised that it could drag more than it could carry.

From sledges, there came clumsy solid wooden-wheeled vehicles until the spoke and axle led to the more elegant late 19th and 20th century coaches and carriages which comprise those in the Collection today.

At the present time the exhibits include several passenger-carrying vehicles, two fire engines and a game van. Unfortunately, as in the case of the cycles, they have no known active past other than their common use, and in some cases also their origins are obscure.

A one-time exhibit of the Collection is a Barouche of the 1870 period, and although it is no longer on view it took pride of place as it was the carriage used at the marriages of both the grandparents and parents of Richard Shuttleworth. It was essentially a 'town' carriage and used mostly for dress occasions and with its shallow saucer-like body of elegant lines it was usually driven by a coachman in livery who was accompanied by a groom. This version is the two-horse kind, but there were other versions which were drawn by as many as six horses as the occasion demanded.

Moving into the next decade, 1880 sees the Private or Park Coach, or Drag as it is sometimes called. It has been said that a four-masted ship in sail and a four-in-hand coach at speed compare with the epitome of grace and beauty.

This type of coach owes its origin to the mail and stage coaches of earlier years, and its revival was, in great part, due to the forming of the Four-in-Hand driving club in 1856. The Shuttleworth exhibit is typical of the coach of the period and it provided an excellent grandstand at race meetings and similar gatherings. It is very well equipped, especially at the rear where there is a boot containing drawers and other receptacles. Despite being one of the most admired of the passenger-carrying exhibits, little is known about it other than it is believed to have been owned by the Shuttleworth family.

Another exhibit of the same period is the Brougham carriage which took its name from Lord Brougham, to whom is attributed the idea of the particular style which was introduced in about 1839. Most of the carriages of the time were beyond the means of business and professional men, so there arose a need for a closed vehicle which could be drawn by one horse, and which was less expensive. The Brougham was built with that in mind. As the vehicle stands today its roadworthiness is questionable, so along with some of the other carriages it awaits its turn for restoration. This item, too, is thought to have been owned by the Shuttleworth family.

At the turn of the century another vehicle, the Gig, was gaining rapid popularity, and one is in the Collection. This type of two-wheeled carriage found its popularity among those who liked to drive themselves and get around quickly — farmers, commercial travellers and businessmen. Travel by road was the only practicable way for these people, and the Gig provided the answer. Many owners had their private Gig house as one has a garage today. Little is known of this vehicle's past.

In 1902 the American Buggy made its appearance and one once owned by the Shuttleworth family is on view. It is recorded that Colonel Shuttleworth always drove it with a very fast pony. The term Buggy as used in this country was meant to denote a hooded Gig, since it belonged to the Gig family. It has certain advantages over the Gig in that its passengers are comfortably seated and shielded from the sun and rain while at the same time open to the air. This item is in a good state of preservation.

The Dog Cart of around 1904 is another of the range of the Shuttleworth's horse-drawn vehicles. It is a 'country' rather than a 'town' vehicle, and was designed for carrying gun dogs or greyhounds with their owners to sports meetings. The body consists of a square box, often with ventilation louvres for the dogs, with back-to-back seating for four persons. Quite frequently it was used as a general-purpose cart.

Time has revealed that of all the horsedrawn vehicles in the Collection, the Governess Cart of 1907 is the one which shares with the coach the admiration of all visitors for its simplicity and quiet elegance. It is a low-built carriage, and was used mostly in the country for the conveyance of children and old folk. It is fitted with a door at the rear, and seats about four people with their backs to the wheels and facing each other. Driving is done from the back on the off side, a position which is not ideal, thus requiring a pony of placid temperament. It is in a very good state of preservation.

The last, but not the least of the passenger-carrying vehicles is the Pony Phaeton, also of the 1907 period. It can be drawn by either a pony or a donkey. Mrs. Shuttleworth used it on many occasions to take young Richard on outings, and because of the lack of seating space he had to sit facing his mother's knees. It is still quite good in appearance, but some work is required on parts which have perished.

The Game Van in the Collection is a relatively little-known form of transport and its caravan-like appearance arouses a lot of curiosity. It is a relative of the dog cart and was used for the storage of dead birds during organised shoots, and in a secondary role of holding extra protective clothing. The big cab seats three and has locker and coat-hanger space and the box-like body 4ft by 4ft 6ins by 5ft 10ins high is equipped with a system of sliding bars capable of taking between 400 and 500 hung birds. The van is ventilated and lockable.

Shuttleworth's example was made in about 1904 by Percy Heaton of Stetchworth, Newmarket, and an exactly similar vehicle was supplied to King Edward VII. Although no records of its early history exist, it appears to have needed no attention during its long life except cleaning and painting.

The two horsedrawn fire engines in the Collection are a Merryweather Greenwich of about 1906 and a Shand Mason New Volunteer of about 1913. Apart from many differences in boiler and other items, the two engines are much alike in basic configuration. After so many years of disuse it is unlikely that they are in working order, and their appearance suggests that a considerable amount of work is needed in order to restore them to a reasonable condition. (In the early 1920s the firm of Shand

Mason was taken over by Merryweather). The Shand Mason engine displays the name Ampthill, which is assumed to be the local authority who originally owned it, and it is believed that one of the two was used on the Shuttleworth estate.

Motorcars:

The Shuttleworth Collection is best known for its aircraft, although Richard bought his first car in 1928 before he had acquired an aeroplane. Today the Collection has 16 cars and, of the 13 exhibited, 11 are owned by the Shuttleworth Collection and two are on long-term loan.

All the cars in the Collection are renowned in one way or another, some in more ways than one, but the one which has the lion's share of fame is the Panhard Levassor, as in addition to all else it is the first car which Richard Shuttleworth purchased and so began the Collection.

He bought it in 1928 from Lord Rothchild's chauffeur for the princely sum of 25 shillings (£1.25p). The car is of the 1898 period, and although 1898 is almost certain to be the correct one, the accuracy of the date is sometimes challenged. To those who come to see elegance on wheels the actual date will not be important.

It was the first four-cylinder car to be built by Panhard, and its treasury rating is 12 hp. There are four forward and four reverse gears, and side chains for the final drive. At the rear, a device known as a sprag is fitted to prevent the car from rolling backwards on an incline.

Richard Shuttleworth drove the exhibit in the 1928 London-Brighton car run and completed the course non-stop, thus proving its continued reliability, such as it showed in the 890-mile race from Paris to Amsterdam in 1898 in which it came fourth, having completed the course at an average speed of 24 mph. It also took part in the London-Brighton car run in 1929, in 1931; and again in 1978. It is of further interest that in addition to being owned by Lord Rothschild, the exhibit is reputed to have been used by King Edward VII to go to Ascot races.

In its present condition it is a paragon of elegance and a tribute to the standard of the work of restoration. To detail all the work that has been done would be too lengthy, but it can be summarised by saying that the car has been almost rebuilt from the engine to the upholstery.

Another car produced by one of the pioneer makers of the same period is the Benz International. Unlike the Panhard, it has no notable achievement to claim, but it was Benz, its maker, who

Treadle drive Boneshaker 1860.

Locomobile Steam Car 1901.

Baby Peugeot 1902.

Pony Phaeton 1907.

is recognised generally as being the first to make a car of such practical value that production on a commercial scale was worthwhile.

The car has a single-cylinder engine of 3 hp, on the side of which is a 20in-diameter flywheel that must be rotated manually for starting. Owing to the direction of rotation of the engine, the driving belt from the engine to the countershaft is crossed in order to give the car its forward motion. There are three forward speeds but no reverse, and final drive is to the rear wheels by side chains from the counter shaft. The exhibit has recently made its appearance again after a long spell in the workshops, where it underwent an amount of restoration tantamount to a complete rebuild. The Benz took part in the London-Brighton run in 1932, 1934 and 1936.

The Mors 'Petit Duc' is a car also of the period 1899. It is at present the Cinderella of the cars on show due to the need for a great deal of attention. In addition to the extent of work required on the body, the absence of the engine makes the task of complete restoration even more formidable. The two-cylinder 5 hp engine was removed some years ago with the intention of making it usable again, but its condition was such that it appeared to be beyond reprieve. Since then it has become but a memory. The car is a two seater fitted with a collapsible dicky seat at the rear.

In spite of its delapidated condition there is one aspect of life that attracts interest. An entry on the certificate issued by the Veteran Car Club reads: '*Makers stamped hub caps. A letter dated 1930 signed by the original owner states that the car was purchased in Paris in September 1899 price £262-00-0 and it was delivered to the owner, the Rev R.V.O. Graves, vicar of Tolleshunt D'Archy, Essex, in the first week of October 1899 by Frank Wellington. The car took part in the London-Brighton run in 1900. It was registered by the Rev Graves on the 1st January 1904 and allotted the number F7, the previous six Essex numbers being reserved by the authorities at Chelmsford for official vehicles. Thus it is the first private car registered in Essex. Attempts are now being made to locate the Rev Graves if he is still alive.*'

There is also a touch of humour on the same document in the form of question and answer. Q No. 25. Is a starter fitted? A ...Driver's Elbow!

Entering the next decade, the Arrol Johnston of 1901 is the earliest of the exhibits. The Arrol Johnston cars were originally made and marketed by the MO-CAR Syndicate of Paisley, but in about 1905 the firm became the Arrol Johntson Motor Car

Company. The Dog Cart was their first design and one which remained very popular in its place of origin despite massive proportions and huge solid-tyred wheels. The exhibit is a six-seater and was produced in 1901. It has a horizontally opposed two-cylinder water-cooled engine in which each cylinder has two pistons with a common combustion chamber, between each pair of piston heads. It is also fitted with a water injector, which enables it to replenish the cooling system from pools and other sources. The Treasury rating for the engine is 12 hp.

While such a vehicle might appear ungainly and even unconventional by the standards of the time, especially with the driver positioned in a seat behind the front passengers, it took part in the Glasgow Autocar Trials of September 1901. A measure of its performance and reliability is highlighted by the fact that after completing a course of 500 miles it came in first, without losing a mark.

It was collected by Richard Shuttleworth from Dumfries in December 1931 and driven 250 miles to Old Warden. Although it is still in working order it looks a little forlorn, but a little 'spit and polish' will do much to enhance its appearance when time permits.

Another unusual car of the 1901 period is the Steam Locomobile, and much could be written about it and its origin. It is a two-seater and one of the first American light steamers. It was made by The Locomobile Company of America to a design of the Stanley Brothers whose patent rights it acquired. Later, it was marketed in this country by the Locomobile Company of Great Britain. The Treasury rating of the two-cylinder engine is $5\frac{1}{2}$ hp. It is flexible and reversible and has no gears. It has tiller steering, original single-tube tyres fitted to wire-spoke wheels, and a final drive by a central chain to the rear axle. The motive mechanism assembly (boiler, water tank, pressurised fuel tank, engine and silencing drum) is almost completely housed below the seat and in the boot.

The present attractive appearance and performance of the vehicle are again the results of much painstaking work, especially in the case of the boiler which has been retubed. The comprehensive restoration has included not only the engine and boiler but the wheels, upholstery, and the paintwork. When new it cost £190. It took part in the London-Brighton car run in 1937 and 1938; in the 1937 run it was disqualified for arriving too early.

The Baby Peugeot of 1902 is another of the Collection's favourites which attracts a great deal of attention from visitors of

146

all ages. It is a small two-seater which was used in large numbers in the early years of this century. Fitted with a 5 hp single-cylinder engine, it is capable of about 28-30 mph. It has three forward speeds and one reverse together with an interesting feature of design for the period in that the final drive to the rear wheels is by bevel gears, a significant departure from the chain drive of its contemporaries, but a successful one.

The exhibit is a splendid example of design, workmanship and forward thinking of the time; the reputation established by the makers still exists today. As with many of the other car exhibits, time has taken its toll, and a considerable amount of work on the engine and body has been necessary to restore the car to its present resplendent condition. From 1929 it has taken part in many London-Brighton runs and is still competing after 29 runs.

Another of Richard Shuttleworth's acquisitions is the De Dietrich of 1903, then an expensive car at £976. Although it has not got the elegance of the Panhard it has a unique attraction of its own in the form of a robust and rugged appearance. It is fitted with a four-cylinder 24 hp engine, three forward speeds and one reverse, a final drive by side chains to the rear wheels, a racing body with bucket seats, and Stepney wheels. The restoration work required on both body and engine of this exhibit was also very extensive. Like many of the other cars in the Collection the De Dietrich has taken part in several London-Brighton runs since 1928, the last entry in 1978 making a recorded total of 19.

The largest car in the range of exhibits is a Crossley of 1912. It is a six-seat open tourer with a folding hood and fitted with a four-cylinder engine of 14 hp. The chassis is robust and durable, and it was this durability which gained for the firm of Crossley a contract with the War Office during the 1914-18 war. The Crossley chassis of the day was standard for light tenders, mobile workshops, ambulances and Staff cars, which were used in large numbers by the Royal Flying Corps. The Crossley was presented to the Collection by the magazine Flight, and its state of preservation is such that it should not need any major attention for a long time to come.

The Morris Oxford of 1913 is an early example of that famous and popular car. The engine is a 10 hp four-cylinder White & Poppe, water cooled and with magneto ignition. There are three forward speeds and one reverse, and the rear end of the gearbox carries a housing for the spherical end of the propeller shaft casing. From the gearbox the drive is transmitted by an enclosed propeller shaft to a worm-drive rear axle. The introduction of worm gearing for rear-wheel drive was at the time something quite new. A noteworthy feature of this little car is the entire enclosure of the transmission, thereby affording complete protection from dust. The body is a two seater with a dicky seat.

In addition to the Shuttleworth-owned cars described here, a 1904 De Dion and an Adams-Hewitt of 1906 (built in Bedford) are on loan to the Collection and on view to visitors.

Finally a vehicle with special aviation associations is the Hucks starter. In the early days of flying, many aircraft engines were of comparatively low power, so it was easy and customary to start them by swinging the propeller. As engine design progressed resulting in increased power, starting soon presented a problem, especially as propeller swinging became difficult, if not impossible, due, not only to the compression to be overcome, but also to the increase in propeller diameter.

Various methods and devices for starting were tried; some were even adopted on a permanent basis, but the device which was most highly favoured was the Hucks Starter. This derived its name from the originator of the idea, Mr. B.C. Hucks who, amongst other things was one of Britain's early and most famous flyers.

The starter comprises basically a Model "T" Ford car chassis complete with engine and gearbox, on which is erected the structure for the starting mechanism. The mechanism is simple in design, construction, and operation. It consists of a long shaft mounted on a skeleton structure of tubular steel, the shaft being driven by sprockets and chain from the gearbox when the appropriate gearbox drive is engaged.

At the front end, the shaft has a crosshead which engages with a starter dog fitted to the front of the propeller hub. The part of the shaft to which the crosshead is fitted can be moved telescopically against a spring for automatic disengagment once the engine has started. A universal joint enables the crosshead to be aligned with the starter dog on the propeller.

This particular vehicle is not only one of the Collection's unique exhibits, but it is one which still plays an important working part at some of the Flying Displays. It came from the same source as the Bristol Fighter and was rebuilt and restored to its present condition for the Collection by the de Havilland Aircraft Company at their Technical School. The de Havilland company was responsible for the conversion of a large number of Model "T" Ford cars to this particular role.

The horse-drawn vehicles are in need of attention before they are fit for the road; some of the bicyles are in good working order and the intention is that all the cars should run again. Already many of the cars are in very good mechanical condition, as many have undergone extensive restoration during recent years. The others await their turns for places in the work programme, but as with the aeroplanes, the pace of progress is dictated by time, money and available technical resources. Help towards this task has been provided by grants from the Transport Trust.

On special occasions the working vehicles in the Collection emerge for their static positions to be driven or ridden around the aerodrome. Once or twice each year they are joined by others to make up a comprehensive parade of historic transport. Either on their own or displayed in conjunction with the aeroplanes, the cars and bicycles on the move form an important aspect of the Old Warden activity and serve as a reminder of Richard Shuttleworth's earliest endeavours in acquisition, restoration and operation of historic transport items. However, to avoid duplication of exhibits and to provide space for improving the overall layout, a few of the horse-drawn vehicles and bicycles are to be withdrawn from the Collection; thus a more balanced range of items will be displayed.

Chapter 9
The Long Task of Restoration

by Chris Morris

Chris Morris served his apprenticeship with de Havilland at Hatfield, rebuilt several Tiger Moths whilst with Bowker Air Services and joined the Collection's engineering staff in 1980. Now he is the Chief Inspector, with particular responsibility for restoration of the famous de Havilland Comet that won the England to Australia air race in 1934.

When you see a historic aeroplane being wheeled onto the airfield, or standing very smartly on the flight line before taking its turn in a flying display, or just sitting statically on normal everyday exhibition, remember that many years may have been spent on fact-finding research, in restoration and in seeking components to enable the machine to be in its present state.

No two aeroplanes are alike; this complicates the problem, for the job of re-building a sole surviving example of a type that may have ceased production nearly half a century before means that no parts can be drawn from the stores against a signature, or bought on the stockists shelves, or even ordered from anywhere. Quite often a part may be the subject of a world-wide search through a network of contacts, sometimes on a mutual exchange basis. This may take two or three years, perhaps with fruitless results, at the end of which everyone must admit that such an item cannot be traced in any country. Then follows the problem of an alternative supply source. The only answer lies in building-up the defective part, using it as a pattern, and the making a new item; but what if the item is missing altogether so that there is no base from which to build afresh? Working drawings, of course, provide the easiest solution, but what are the chances of finding such luxuries after so many years? Slim. Although occasionally they can be found, in by far the majority of cases they have disappeared many years previously; and so the difficulties mount.

So let us look now at a few recent projects. One good case for treatment is the Hawker Hind light bomber of 1937. This very significant historic aeroplane was presented to the Collection by the (then Royal) Afghan Air Force and, following a formal hand-over ceremony at Kabul airport, was driven home to England on an overland journey of 6,000 miles. It was sufficiently complete to be assembled for the handover and again on arrival in England, where it stood proudly in the car park of the Ford Motor Company's headquarters at Warley in Essex. There it was photographed for every national daily newspaper and for a number of other publications, appearing to all as though it was an aeroplane that would need little more than fuel, oil and coolant to enable it to be started and flown. How wrong such an appearance can be!

The Hind lay dismantled at Old Warden for a considerable time before a serious investigation could be carried out, but then every component was inspected, labelled and earmarked for repair, rebuild or rejection. Here the ever-present problem of deciding what part can be used and what part must be replaced causes perpetual headaches to the technical staff, for the aim is to retain as many original parts as possible and yet produce an aeroplane that will be safe to fly for many years ahead. This leads to perpetual conflict between a person's left and right hands.

As has been said, the detailed investigation (the Preliminary Investigation Report) was completed, looking into the structural

The Bristol Fighter being dismantled for major overhaul, re-cover and repaint, a task carried out in 1981-82.

integrity of the fuselage, engine bearers, undercarriage, wing spars, fittings, struts, for internal corrosion, cracks and distortion, and all the moving and working parts that are attached to the structure. At the same time outside firms, organisations and libraries were contacted for the specialist knowledge required to carry out these tasks. Rolls Royce, for instance, came down from Glasgow to have a detailed look at (and in) their Kestrel engine, but without major dismantling. Then they drew up a very comprehensive 'Prelim' of their own for the Collection's engineers to work through, with a detailed maintenance schedule attached to their report for continued serviceability for the future. Hawker Siddeley, of Kingston, successors to the designers and makers of the Hind, were able to supply photocopies of a large number of working drawings, which helped considerably. Shuttleworth staff were able to check, repair or remanufacture several items from these drawings, as (of necessity) the drawings contain a great deal of information in themselves. The RAF Museum Library section at Hendon was able to supply copies of the original Air Publications (A.Ps. for short); these were (and still are) the RAF's 'Bible' of information to ensure continued airworthiness of the aircraft and associated matters. They are drawn up jointly by the manufacturers and the Services, and those in which the Collection was interested related to the airframe (rigging, repairs, maintenance schedules etc) engine and related equipment. Also the RAF Museum was able to help in another very important way, for Hendon had a complete former Afghan Air Force Hind on static exhibition. An excellent rapport was established with the Keeper of Aircraft, for either borrowing an item for re-manufacture, or exchanging an item, or in one case only, the outright loan of an item, where one was missing. What problems there would have been without this help, as there are only two other known Hinds in the world, both incomplete!

Now that the contacts had been established, the time had come to make a physical start. After the strip, inspection and orderly work schedule had been compiled and agreed between the Collection's engineers and the Civil Aviation Authority, the real work began. An immediate task (this was in 1972-73) was to replace all the wood work on the fuselage, which runs from aft of the engine to the tail. This gives shape to the fuselage and protection to the crew, and is not a part of the load-bearing structure. The shape was there under the fabric covering, but was

The Bristol Fighter taking shape again in 1982 after a major overhaul and repaint.

literally a 'lash up' of commercial TV-aerial-type aluminium tubing, Russian tea cases and timber of very suspect origin. Many people participated in this complete task, for not only did various Shuttleworth apprentices cut their teeth (and fingers) on the delicate woodwork and pattern-making involved, but a talented S.V.A.S. member gave a considerable amount of his time! Another spur was that the RAF's Hind was being made museum worthy a few miles away at Henlow and Cardington, giving an ideal opportunity to compare notes and glean ideas.

The fuselage and cockpit woodwork was only one integral part of the whole project. Numerous firms, small and not so small gave time and expertise to overhaul items. Individuals, too, gave a considerable amount of time and energy, repairing and remaking most of the polished engine cowlings, remaking coolant, oil and fuel pipes; the list is almost a who's who in the aviation world, beaten only by the help received subsequently in the greatest of all projects — the 1934 de Havilland Comet.

With the best plans and timetable in the world, on a project such as this, it is not impossible to put an accurate timetable on

The Hawker Hind with fuselage stripped, but with the basic structure repaired and reprotected. A dilapidated Bristol Fighter fuselage hangs from the roof behind.

The Hind: Structural progress advances.

The Hind, refurbished, re-covered and repainted, awaits its wings.

Achievement: The rebuilt Hind about to be test-flown by Wing Commander R. F. (Dick) Martin.

anything. Most outside help is of a voluntary nature and work has to be carried out in available time to fit in with other schedules. One firm took several small items to overhaul and then won a major international order, which became bad news for the Hind project initially, but good news for them! Another company looked at the radiator for the Kestrel — about 200 lbs of copper tubing, brass sheet and solder, and had to give a commercial quote, quite outside the Collection's pocket. A small firm in London agreed to undertake the work, held on to the radiator for a couple of years and then admitted their inability to complete the task. Then a very sympathetic vintage radiator specialist in Cambridge gave an acceptable quote and a realistic time scale, which meant that it would be ready only just before the schedule time for completion of the airframe. Things were getting tight! An appeal for funds was sent to members of the Shuttleworth Veteran Aeroplane Society and response was very encouraging; the radiator was made, delivered, fitted, filled, declared 100% watertight, and the Hind went straight into engine runs and a flight test schedule, to appear in the air on the last flying day of 1981. There was still a small rectification, alteration and adjustment programme to do in the winter of 1981/82, but all the hard work, outside help and enthusiasm had been moulded together to complete one more historic aircraft for the unique range of Shuttleworth 'living' exhibits.

The Comet project has been quoted as being the world's largest rebuilding task, taking into the account the man-hours, cost, and number of outside firms involved. This report may not totally convince you that this is so, but talk to anyone on the project, and your views will surely be changed! The history of this particular aircraft is documented well elsewhere, but so far the story of the refurbishing side has not been told in full.

The project to bring G-ACSS to flying condition really started in late 1973 with a very good inspection of the structure, taking into account its previous storage life of sitting on a coastal airfield under a damp tarpaulin cover for several years, being lightened, drilled and slung high in a roof at the Festival of Britain, and later again being slung in another heated roof. All of these conditions are extremely bad for a completely wood and glue structure, so everyone expected the worst on opening up. The wing was removed from the fuselage and laid upsidedown on special trestles to keep its shape; then the bottom face (now the top) cross planking skinning was systematically removed, until the total inside structure of ribs, spars and fittings could be inspected and repaired or replaced as required. Then the next long task of reskinning back to its original manufacturers' condition was carried out, the wing job alone taking a year or two.

Whilst the wing was being rebuilt, a complete list was made of all the missing components and drawings. Because of the requirement of minimum weight for slinging in the Fetival of Britain roof in 1951, all components and controls were removed and thrown away (where, oh where is that skip now?). The fuel and oil tanks, support fittings, hoses; the major portions of the engines, their attachment fittings, carburettors, castings, some engine cowling pieces, all the throttle controls and their pulleys and brackets; all the cockpit flying controls, the elevator and rudder trim controls; the handbrake lever, cables, pulleys, brackets, and routings; all the instruments; cabling, drives, routings and engine fittings; cockpit controls including the throttles, cables and most pulleys and brackets; the hot/cold air controls, the pitch and mixture controls and brackets, the seats, their attachments to the structure and the harness attachment

The intricate curvature of the planking that forms such a major portion of the Comet's structure. This shows a fuselage section, but it is used also in the wings.

point and hardware, the cockpit canopy (as the one that came with the aircraft had been "made up" in its non-flying career); parachutes and seat cushions; the tailwheel/skid unit, pilot static head and lines, controls cables and swaged rods; mainwheels, tyres, tubes, brake units; fire extinguisher system and so on. For most of the items, no drawings existed, or at best, sketches in 'Flight' magazines of the period. Positioning of these components is often not known, so the engineers must revert to sketches or a clean sheet, and start again. When a pattern or mock-up had been made of a particular area, it was drawn up, stressed, and then made, by British Aerospace at Hatfield, at Old Warden, or by a sympathetic outside supplier. Each deficiency mentioned entailed at least one outside firm, and sometimes more, with several firms working together to complete a system or article. A designer at Hatfield has given up most of his free time, and by arrangement with the Company, a not inconsiderable amount of company time, to design, draw, have stressed, and have manufactured the missing components. Without him, the whole task would have been almost impossible.

A great deal of planning went into all this, from the earliest initial thoughts on the feasibility of the task, contacting organisations and individuals into which way they can or cannot help, right through the project to the final phase of assembly, ground running and flight. It is quite a task trying to co-ordinate the completion dates of work in hand to the dates required by the firm or firms involved. Like house buying, a small hiccup in a chain can upset the whole system, with a fresh start taking unnecessary time and energy.

To carry on with the structural rebuilding, after the wing was completed, the fuselage was jigged and reskinned along the bottom and the sides of the front portion of the fuselage, keeping the original longeron strength members. The deckings forward of the cockpit, covering the top and bottom of the fuel tanks, (which form part of the rigidity of the structure when bolted in place) were beyond repair, and so these needed to be remade. No drawings existed: not that this would have helped, as they are double-curvatured one sixteenth cross lapped laths of spruce glued together to give an extremely strong monocoque type structure. The only way of re-making them was solved when a close contact in the plastics trade offered to make a large, rigid female fibreglass mould, weighing several hundredweight, in which to lay and glue the laths, the bulkheads and stringers to

The complex planking that covers the Comet's wing between the first and rear spars has been completed. The first part of the ply leading edge is being held in position by clamps.

copy the exact shape and size of the old decking. Flushness with the main fuselage structure along its edges was essential, primarily for aerodynamic and also for aesthetic reasons.

The tail surfaces (the fin, rudder, elevators and tailplane) are all plywood covered, with no inspection holes, so that one face had to be stripped off — a slow job just like the wing skin; all hinge fittings needed to be cleaned, inspected, protected and replaced, and then re-skinned. The ailerons were just the same, but the two flaps had to be totally rebuilt to pattern, as there were no drawings of these.

Apart form the structural side of the operations, main components such as engines and propellers were acquired from various sources and then extensively overhauled by outside companies. Altogether more than fifty organisations have been involved in the project and the technical help provided ' in kind' has amounted to more than £100,000 in monetary value. The work would have been impracticable without this support from industry and the list of names of the participating bodies must indicate the historical significance that is attached to the project.

The total task, as a national venture with the Shuttleworth Collection at the core, serves to show some of the best of Britain's past and the names of all firms that have contributed to the cause are displayed prominently on a 'board of appreciation' in No. 6 hangar. At the time of writing, the fiftieth anniversaries of both the birth of the Comet and its success in the MacRobertson Air Race from Mildenhall to Melbourne are close. Late in 1984 will G-ACSS be as much a centre of public attraction as it was half a century earlier?

Although the Hind and the Comet have been described here as prime examples of restoration tasks carried out at Old Warden, they are by no means the only projects of importance. Within the past decade the only surviving Parnall Elf of 1929, the 1937 Miles Magister and de Havilland Tiger Moth have been completely rebuilt for the first time round, whilst the reproduction of the 1910 Bristol Boxkite, the 1918 Bristol Fighter, Richard Shuttleworth's Moth of 1928, the 1931 Avro Tutor and numerous aero engines have received major technical attention by the Collection's staff. Then, of course, there is the more routine but equally important work of maintaining the flying fleet in tip-top airworthy condition, remembering that each aeroplane is different, each has been out of production for many, many years and that no spare parts are available from the store shelves.

What lies ahead? Each time that an addition to the Collection is restored, the work is not over, for it is one more machine that takes time and attention on normal running maintenance throughout its new flying career. Therefore, without increasing the engineering strength (and therefore the cost) there comes a situation in which all available staff capacity is needed for the daily task and none remains available for new projects; so, as the Collection is not endowed with limitless finance from above, some rationalisation is essential to keep the entire operation on a workable scale. Some aircraft may be withdrawn from flying for a few years, but any such plan is based on maintaining a broad spread of airworthy aircraft that cover each era and role in the progress of aviation history. Otherwise, a stalemate would be reached and with such interesting types as the little Southern Martlet of 1929 and one of Richard Shuttleworth's 1931 Desoutters awaiting their turns in the restoration programme, some careful long-term planning is essential. No other organisation in the World aims to restore, maintain and fly such a broad spread of types covering the first fifty years of aircraft development; the challenge has its own appeal, but it is not easy!

Chapter 10
What are they like to Fly — and to Display?

There are several aircraft museums containing a host of very valuable machines that have numerous claims to historical fame, but by far the majority of these have been relegated to permanent roles as static exhibits. Clearly they play significant parts in aeronautical education, especially when easily accessible for viewing in city centres; there they are seen each year by thousands of schoolchildren, many of whom otherwise would know only the airliners of the eighties in which they might be fortunate enough to fly on holiday.

The Shuttleworth Collection, however, is unique. The founder, Richard Shuttleworth, insisted that everything in his possession should be made to work as well as it had done when new. That policy has been continued throughout the Collection's existence and today the Old Warden hangars house the World's only range of airworthy historic aeroplanes dating from soon after the birth of manned flight to World War II and beyond.

Very few people are privileged to fly in any of these valuable aeroplanes, for the amount of flying must be kept to a practical minimum in order to reduce wear and tear on engines, airframes and associated components. With one or two exceptions, a Shuttleworth aeroplane takes to the air only when it needs a test flight or to give a public demonstration. A type such as the Sopwith Pup of 1916 with its short-life rotary engine flies about forty minutes in an average year; the earliest flying machines dating to before World War I do even less. But they are maintained in airworthy condition, to be on show each day as living examples of working machinery, with real oil falling onto real drip trays and a total absence of the dead atmosphere that surrounds an inert exhibit.

Clearly each type has its own characteristics and tends to display its own temperament. An early machine, with warping wings instead of ailerons to provide lateral control, may lack the positive response and feel that we expect from the more conventionally-equipped types. The Bleriot, with its main wheels that caster in either direction, cannot be controlled on the ground without suitably knowledgeable help from peop¹ at the wingtips. The Boxkite must be flown within a very small limiting speed range and turns must be made without slip if height is not to be lost, therefore calling for careful planning when positioning for a display.

This is not the place to give detailed descriptions of the handling features of individual aircraft, as these appear in the companion volume 'From Bleriot to Spitfire', but a general explanation may interest. Few people can relate themselves in any way to one of the World's earliest flying machines, but many readers will be pilots and, even for those who have no practical flying experience, a description of a flight in a hypothetical light aeroplane of the late twenties or early thirties may stimulate the imagination.

Firstly, the weather must be right. The wind must be neither strong nor blustery, for the wing loading of an early aeroplane will be low; this means that there is a fairly large area of lifting surface (wing) for a low total weight. Whilst this will affect its in-flight handling, it will be even more noticeable on the ground, when a gust of wind from one side will not only cause the machine to weathercock into the direction from which the air is blowing, but may lift the wing on that side and even cause the other wing to touch the ground — or worse. Next, the aerodrome must be suitable. Generally the length of available take-off or landing run is not a problem, but its direction is. Nearly all aeroplanes until the mid thirties had relatively little directional control when on the ground, with fixed tailskids and no brakes, so a grass airfield that is as broad as it is long provides the ideal answer if operations are not to be stopped when the wind changes. If all take-offs and landings can be made precisely into wind, without the need to climb or approach over or near to gust-generating trees, then many of the problems disappear.

We are ready to fly. We have checked the documents and have accepted the aeroplane. Chocks are placed in front of the wheels, for while this is a wise precaution even on braked aeroplanes, on the brakeless veterans chocks are essential. Before climbing aboard a pilot carries out an external pre-flight check, ensuring that there is no damage to the fabric, all cowlings are secure and their buttons properly closed, controls move freely, landing and flying wires are correctly tensioned, the propeller has no nicks and many other points of relevance to the safety of flight. This walk-round neither reduces the importance of the preparatory work carried out by the engineers, nor is it a reflection on their skills, but the pilot is wholly responsible for the aeroplane that he accepts to fly and minor damage could have occurred after the machine had been signed-out as technically serviceable and before the flight begins.

The pilot checks his equipment, such as ensuring that his goggles are clean and then mounts his machine, taking care where he treads. He satisfies himself that the cushions are correct for height and for his distance from the rudder pedals (although on some types these are adjustable) and he straps himself in tightly. This is very important, for after being aboard for a few minutes, when the cushions have settled, the straps always become looser than when first secured. Unlike those on modern machines, early harnesses cannot be adjusted without unfastening the entire package and starting again. This is a cumbersome procedure and is better completed while there are no other distractions, such as a running engine to handle.

The two most common starting procedures among aircraft of this era are the hand-swing and the use of a starter-magneto. Taking the first, which is more usual among the lighter types, we have relatively few checks to complete, for cockpits of the time have remarkably few moving controls. Petrol on, ignition switches off and throttle closed are the pilot's actions before the engineer floods the carburettor and turns the engine through about four compresssions to suck the fuel into the system. Then, with the stick hard back to prevent the tail from lifting off the ground, the pilot responds to the words "throttle set — contact" by inching the lever slightly forward, turning on the switch(es) and repeating the same words. When the propeller is swung by hand, he makes every endeavour to "catch" the engine as it fires and he gently manipulates the throttle to establish a smooth warm-up setting in the region of 900-1000 rpm. Immediately he checks that the oil pressure is rising. This is perhaps the most important cockpit information available to a pilot and if the pressure fails to increase quickly, he switches off the engine to avoid possible damage through lack of lubrication. Here a pilot requires specialist knowledge of the type, for required oil pressure figures vary from as little as 5 - 8 lbs for a splash-fed system to more than 80 lbs for the average radial.

The alternative starting method, commonly found on Armstrong-Siddeley radials such as the Mongoose in the Hawker Tomtit and the Lynx in the Avro Tutor, but also on the V-8 Airdisco on the DH 51, is by use of a starter-magneto. As a part of airworthiness approval all aero engines are required to have fully duplicated ignition, with two magnetos and with two sparking plugs in each cylinder, but in effect this method includes a third ignition switch connected to a hand-cranked (third) magneto, operated by the pilot, while an engineer winds on the outside to rotate the engine. To ensure that both parties wind at the same time, the order is "one, two, three — go", leading to quite energetic exercise for both. The third switch is turned off as soon as everything is running smoothly.

An aero engine requires a gentle warming-up period, the length depending on the temperature of the day and whether it was a start from cold. If so, even in warm weather, almost five minutes should be allowed to ensure that the oil is not too viscous to be circulating fully before the power is increased for magneto checks. Some engines have oil temperature gauges and on a really cold day twelve minutes can elapse before the minimum operating figure shows on the dial. The warm-up and subsequent running on the ground should not be performed with the engine idling, for this tends to cause plug-fouling, so a compromise setting in the region of 1000 rpm is about right for most machines. This time is not wasted, however, for the pilot carries out checks on instruments, flying controls, trimmer and other essentials for safe flight.

After the engine checks, the chocks can be waved away and taxying begins. This is where we find one of the first main differences in required technique between the ancient and the modern. The older "taildragger" has its nose well above the horizon and therefore offers no view directly forward, so the pilot must weave from side to side throughout the ground manoeuvring stage, swinging the nose to the left and looking to the right to check the ground ahead and then vice versa; but an aeroplane with a tailskid fixed to the sternpost and with no brakes may not always move readily in the required direction. It has a strong desire always to head into wind, so to oppose that natural inclination it may be necessary to use a careful burst of throttle to move some air past the rudder in order to achieve any directional response. However, this calls for caution in two other ways; rapid throttle opening may make the tail lift (possibly causing the propeller to nick the ground, with expensive consequences) and any increase in power will cause the speed to rise, with no brakes available to prevent the machine running away. A part of the vintage art that has died with modernity is the use of ailerons to help to activate a turn; for example, when travelling downwind, a down-going aileron will catch the wind from behind and will help to move that side forward or vice versa when taxying into wind. In confined spaces or when the wind is energetic, wing-tip men are essential; they are not just there for the walk (or trot) but must pull back when on the inside of a turn and must remember to release the pressure before the aircraft reaches the desired new heading, or it will continue well past the pilot's intended direction. Without brakes, taxying downwind or downhill calls for a completely closed throttle, which in turn can lead to plug problems!

We have reached the downwind end of the aerodrome and we carry out some straight-forward but very important pre-take-off checks, amounting mainly to the trim setting, fuel (on and sufficient), oil pressure, hatches, harness and goggles. Here a final dead-cut ignition check is wise, followed by a thorough search all round (especially in the direction of the landing approach) to see that all is clear; but this is a fundamental decision time, especially with a valuable historic aeroplane. If the oil pressure is in doubt, or the engine is not as smooth as it was last time, or the wind is freshening beyond expectations, or for any reason there is not total cockpit contentment, that essential sense of responsibility must always dictate the next move. It is far better to abandon the flight before it begins, to ensure another chance, rather than to regret an unwise decision a little later, even if this entails disappointing a crowd at a flying display. To turn round and taxy back in such a circumstance may be difficult, but probably the aeroplane is the world's last airworthy specimen of its type. The pilot is captain of his own ship; he has been entrusted with a very special piece of machinery and he must act accordingly.

We will assume, though, that all is well and we are ready to go. After a final look round inside the cockpit and another check outside in all directions, we move forward gently to align the aeroplane into wind; then we run ahead slowly for a few yards before opening the throttle, smoothly but fully, easing the stick carefully forward to raise the tail to improve the directional control by putting the rudder more fully into the airflow. During this stage, and especially due to the gyroscopic effect as the tail rises, energetic footwork may be needed in order to keep straight against the torque and propeller slipstream effects, but as the forward speed increases all the controls become more effective and the movements must be progressively reduced. Most machines fly themselves off when ready and few need more than a gentle back pressure to take to the air.

There are various techniques for the climb. Some pilots raise the nose fairly soon after lift-off to establish a steepish climb angle, but this means that the airspeed will be relatively low, with ineffective flying controls, the chance of inadequate engine cooling and the worst possible forward view; also if the engine should fail at an early stage in the climb, the chances of recovery are slim. A more shallow angle and higher airspeed, though, will reduce the rate of climb, so clearly a compromise is wise, but in the case of an historic aeroplane safety and sense must take precedence over performance.

Rudder plays a very significant part in handling a biplane. During the climb, considerable pressure on one pedal must be maintained in order to achieve and sustain balanced flight, the amount depending on the speed and power used and the appropriate side depending on the direction of rotation of the engine. Even in level flight, rudder must be used throughout if the needles of the turn and slip indicator are to show balanced flight.

On many modern aeroplanes, a tolerable (if not very accurate) turn can be achieved by aileron alone, but in our earlier machine sideways stick movement may introduce the required bank but no rate of turn, or even possibly a change of heading in the wrong direction! This is because a downgoing aileron generates more drag than its opposite number. The problem is most marked with the very early designs, on which the downgoing control moves as far as the other moves up, thus creating excessive aileron drag. Later types have differential ailerons, with the upward movement more pronounced than the downward travel, but even with these aids a turn without the use of adequate rudder can be a most ineffective and uncomfortable activity. The best way for a pilot to acquire the art and feel of balanced flight is to practise turns from one direction to the other without pausing in between, but checking the position of the top needle throughout the exercise.

With appropriate respect for their ages, many Shuttleworth aeroplanes are not cleared to perform aerobatic manoeuvres. However some may be looped and one or two are rolled, so long as a positive loading is retained throughout. In the main, a biplane flies round a loop fairly readily, with a need for varying rudder pressures throughout to compensate for changes in the combination of power in relation to airspeed. Some biplanes, though, are reluctant to roll, with the added problem of aileron drag to make the maneouvre a critical performance. Aerobatics, however, are not essential for the enjoyment of pure flying. An open cockpit, the splendid isolation of being alone in the sky with no radio to disturb one's peace of mind and a newly-mown all grass aerodrome are some of the ingredients in the best of the freedom of flight.

One aspect that is of considerable concern to a pilot and of interest to a spectator is the landing. Again, many a modern tricycle machine can be set-up on a steady, powered approach and it is possible (though not correct) to continue this state until the mainwheels touch, then to close the throttle and later apply the brakes. This may be a slight over simplification, but such machines have been landed quite safely in that manner! Not so, though, with the classic taildragging brakeless biplane; here a well-organised approach is essential, a landing path into wind should be selected and the final stages should be made at a predetermined airspeed with stick loads trimmed out. If the approach is too high, there are no flaps to act as drag-producing barn doors, so sideslipping is the only way in which the surplus height can be shed. This is an art that few pilots practise — and none learn — today, but on the glide one wing is lowered and opposite rudder is applied to prevent the nose from falling, therefore presenting much more aeroplane into the oncoming airflow and causing a steeper descent without an embarassing increase in airspeed. When the desired glide path is reached again, the wings are levelled and the rudder centralised to resume a normal glide, but the change of flight condition must be completed at a safe height; this is to avoid either sideslipping into the ground or causing too many tasks to be carried out at the same time, for the airspeed, height and angle of hold-off are critical if a tidy and safe landing is to be achieved on all three points.

A pilot should look well ahead when landing any type of aircraft, but his point of vision is more critical with a taildragger, as he must assess the correct angle at which to touch down by relation to the amount of nose that appears above the horizon. This varies vastly from one type to another, so it is wise to have a mental picture of the amount of aeroplane that you require to see ahead. The airspeed at the start of the hold-off and the rate at which this is performed are equally critical, for either too high a figure or too rapid a round out (or, worse still, both!) will cause the aircraft to gain height and then "sit up and beg" with a rapid loss of both airspeed and control. Too late or too gentle a hold-off, though, is less punitive, for this can be converted into a safe if possibly untidy landing on the mainwheels only, provided that the tail has been lowered sufficiently to ensure adequate ground clearance for the propeller. On some types, though, this clearance is small and a virtual three-pointer is almost essential.

Once an aeroplane is on the ground on all three points, the only causes for it to become airborne again are a patch of rough ground or a severe gust. Such an unexpected excursion into the air is not a handling fault by the pilot. With a wheel landing, though, the pilot must take care not to ease the stick back until the tail is ready to go down of its own accord, for in this case the machine has been placed on the ground at something more than the minimum flying speed, so it is ready to take to the air again briefly at the slightest touch of pilot provocation. Obviously some aircraft are easier than others to place neatly onto three points, while all are susceptible to the effects of the conditions of the moment. In a calm, most machines can be positioned accurately onto the ground with a gentle but satisfying 'clunk', but strong and especially gusty winds can play havoc with any pilot's best-laid plans. In such circumstances, or if it is necessary to land out of wind, an intentional wheeler is a cautious move.

Another significant difference between a tail-down and a tricycle type concerns the nature of the landing run. Apart from a need to prevent over-running the end of the airfield (for, with less aerodynamic drag in its level ground attitude a 'trike' tends to roll further) the more modern machine calls for relatively little pilot attention. On a three point landing, though, smart reactions may be necessary, especially as the speed decreases and the lowered rudder has very little passing airflow to make it effective. Here, a complete calm can be more embarassing than a gentle steady wind, for just prior to stopping, with no brakes and virtually no moving air, even rapid and maximum rudder deflection may have little effect. This is the time at which a swing is most likely to start, with the pilot having the minimum chance of being able to prevent it from developing into a ground loop. The problem is accentuated on a tail-down type because, to make the tail of the aircraft sit on the ground, the centre of gravity must be behind the main wheels, so when a swing starts, the momentum is such that the bulk of the aircraft's weight tends to push ahead and aggravate the swing. By this stage the pilot may be wise to admit temporary defeat, for he will have little control over whether the aeroplane comes gradually to a gentle halt or whether the turn tightens sufficiently severely to cause a side-strain on the undercarriage or even cause the outside wing to dip into the ground. While most flight phases should be in the control of the pilot, this situation must be accepted as one of the less happy moments in the life of anyone who flies tail-dragging (and especially brakeless) historic aeroplanes. Fortunately serious groundloops are rare, but they do and will happen — even to the best!

We will assume that the landing, if not perfect, has ended normally. The flight as such may be over, but the sortie is not. The aircraft must be returned safely to dispersal, using wing-tip handlers if the type and/or conditions make it wise to do so. It must be parked correctly and sensibly, remembering that unaided turns cannot be made in confined spaces and that there are no brakes with which to stop. Finally, although most people remember to warm and run-up an engine before flying, many tend to overlook the need for careful handling at the end. Types vary, but to ensure even cooling and to clear the plugs after taxying most power units should be given a steady run-down for several minutes before switching off.

After turning off the fuel, ensuring that **all** switches are off and completing any other post-flight checks, a pilot should have a few words with an engineer to discuss any points that may be relevant. Was the oil pressure steady throughout the flight? Were there any rough spots on the engine at any power setting? Was the rigging right with the wings level in stick central/hands off cruising flight? A previous pilot had reported a sticking gauge; had the action taken cured this? If anything of special significance was noticed this should be recorded in writing, for tendencies over several flights, probably by different pilots, could tell a tale that might prevent trouble developing in the future.

Apart from entering the flight details in the authorisation book, the pilot has completed the exercise. He can relax and think back. Perhaps he has first flown the world's sole surviving specimen of a famous historic type; both before and during the trip he was aware of the responsibility that goes with this. It should not have prevented him from deriving his ration of pleasure, but only now can he savour the full effects of vintage-style aviation. One experienced pilot stated that flying was really enjoyable only in retrospect, but that the pleasures of taking the thoughts of the day's flight to the evening armchair, or to the bath, far outweighed any of the worries that may have arisen during the trip itself; but this is another story. The problems and pleasures associated with aeroplanes and flying warrant a special book and this is not the place to reminisce.

*　　*　　*

This brief description of a local sortie in an historic aeroplane may come to life more fully if we consider now a typical demonstration flight, for this is what many thousands of visitors come to Old Warden to see. Some people travel for literally hundreds of miles to watch their chosen aeroplanes in the air and the organisers and pilots are aware of the various wishes of different groups of spectators. Some come to take still photographs, others concentrate on cine shooting, while another group concentrates on making sound recordings of engine starting, or of various power settings in flight, or the crackle that some exhausts emit when throttle is fully closed. These and the wishes of the majority, who wish just to see the machines in the air at close quarters and others who are anxious to hear historical detail over the public address system, are fed into a display pattern that must be dictated primarily by the needs of flight safety.

Preliminary planning for any but the smallest flying display must begin many months before the day of the event, but from a flying angle a pilot is concerned only from the morning of the show. He will have his aircraft allocated to him and he will begin to consider whether the conditions are likely to affect the nature of his demonstration. If the wind is light and conditions are smooth, he knows that he will have scope to present the machine accurately and manoeuvres will be possible within easy view of the crowd. If there are gusts, he will need added height and may need to make only gently-banked turns avoiding known areas of turbulence. The decision is based not solely on wind strength, for rough-riding thermal activity can occur when the windsock is well below the horizontal.

Before the show starts, all pilots attend a detailed briefing on the afternoon's plan. The weather, any local restrictions or unusual activities are discussed, timings agreed and questions answered. There may be doubts about which grass runway to use, for one heading may suit one type that needs to operate into wind and another may be more suitable for a second machine that requires a longer run. However, these and other matters are resolved, with the proviso that if weather conditions should change just before or during the display, final discussions will take place on the flight line.

The show has begun. We are the third item on the programme and we have an allocation of seven minutes in the air. This could be critical, for the next performer is a visiting aircraft that is operating on an overhead time slot, so if for any reason we should be a minute late in beginning the demonstration, we must reduce our time by this amount unless there has been a mutual pre-flight agreement with all other parties concerned.

The second aircraft in the display is on the far side of the airfield, at the take-off holding point, with two minutes to go, so with ten minutes before our public performance begins it is time for us to be aboard our machine. We must allow for the possibility of a hesitant starter, with adequate time for an unhurried warm-up and run-up and for taxying out while the previous machine is before the crowd. Just as we are about to wave away the chocks, we receive a message that item number 4 will be two minutes late on the overhead slot; we should absorb this by delaying our take-off until the previous machine has landed and cleared the runway and then extend our airborne performance by one minute. We plan how to use this extra time effectively whilst we are taxying to the take-off point.

We are there. The wind is blowing steadily at about 10 knots almost straight down the ruwnay. Good. The previous aircraft is positioning on final approach, lands very tidily, runs straight without undue effort by the pilot because of the convenient wind direction and clears to the right to avoid the need to cross the duty runway whilst taxying back. A glance round the circuit to ensure that there are no intruders, an especial check that the approach is clear, a glance at air traffic control from which a steady green light is trained on us and away we go. Safety before spectacle is the order, so we climb gently ahead over the college sports field to gain airspeed before beginning a turn round the clump of trees, taking care to keep the Home Farm well clear on the outside, leading to a straight run-in, almost downwind along the front but well clear of the public enclosure fence. Not too low, for then only the people in the front would see; but too high and the effect is lost. Just under half throttle, a quick glance at the oil presssure and a gentle power increase before completing a moderately banked right hand turn inside the north end of the airfield, through 360°, then continuing ahead over an empty stretch of the overflow car park on the north side of the Biggleswade road. A slight gain in height is advisable here before a carefully positioned left-hand turn round the trees of the coach part, to begin another flypast from beside the blister hangar, along the first part of the NW-SE grass runway and, with ample airspeed in hand after descending again from the turn round the trees, a steepish right-hand level turn round the outside of the display flight line, well outboard of the air traffic building, but close enough for the cameras to click successfully. The view of the upper surface of the aircraft that this manoeuvre provides seems to be the most popular for spectators and photographers alike.

Still we have some airspeed in hand and we are facing into wind, so we increase power again, raise the nose, and with a quick oil pressure and time check (three and a half minutes to go) carry out a gentle wing-over to the left. This places us near the upwind end of the field, from which we decend downwind along the front of the enclosure again to carry out a steepish climbing turn to the right over the Biggleswade road hedge towards the bridge; but instead of repeating a full wing-over, we level our nose at the highest point heading up the NE-SW runway, which gives us an ideal position and a low airspeed from which to make a well-throttled-back minimum-speed flypast. We have left this until a late stage in the demonstration, for by now we are satisfied that there is virtually no turbulence, no windsheer nor any other meteorological trap for the man who flies both low and slow.

We are at the upwind end and have remained at a constant 200 ft. in our slow run. More power, another tightish turn round the tree clump and a final fastish run downwind leading into a sustained level steep turn to the right, inside the manoeuvring area of the airfield, finishing after 450°, heading over the windsock to the east (checking: one minute left) for a run straight into a shortened, close-in downwind leg, short base and then a landing approach from a short final position. But alas, we have slightly overestimated the wind strength and we need to slip-off some height, but this is no worry for it is an impressive vintage-style manoevure and could well have been an intentional part of the display. No one will know otherwise, although a few pilots might guess and one or two will probably say so. Apart from this minor misjudgement, with calm conditions and a well-mannered aeroplane, the sequence has worked well. Now there is just the landing left to do. Just? This is the one time at which eyes and voices (qualified and otherwise) are at their most critical. Every pilot knows it. With thousands of people in the viewing enclosure we are aware that a hash-up here will be seen, noted and remembered to the extent that any reasonable demonstration flying that may have gone before it will be forgotten immediately. We try hard, but not too hard, for only a relaxed pilot lands well. We touch quite smoothly, but with the tailskid slightly off the ground in what is called a tail-down wheeler. Acceptable, perhaps, but really a sideslipping approach should be followed by a three-pointer. Although other pilots might notice, fortunately the non-flying members of the audience react only to bounces or ballooning, so we are safe from scorn.

The landing run is dead straight, the credit for which must go the wind blowing down the runway, but we are slightly self-critical at failing to land precisely as we intended and this could spoil any post-flight feeling of contentment. However, just as we have turned off the strip at the end of our landing run, item 4 in the programme flies steadily overhead, leaving no gap between the display acts. Was our precise timing through luck, or careful judgement? To compensate for the wheely landing we credit ourself with the latter; and we are happy again.

Although the description of a typical demonstration flight refers to the need for precise timing throughout an event, a change of plan from 1982 has reintroduced informal unhurried minor events that formed the pattern of the open days of the sixties. On these occasions each historic aeroplane starts, taxies, flies and returns to the flight line without any other machine moving. These smaller events are interspersed with a number of large full-scale displays or pageants, therefore providing facilities for visitors of all tastes.

*   *   *

Before moving away from the art of vintage flight, perhaps we should explain that the pilot of a historic aeroplane is not necessarily better or more qualified than one who flies the modern 'tin trike'. The requirements are different. An early aeroplane calls for more in the way of handling and airmanship skills, but there are no avionics or other electronic devices to master; the later machine is much less tricky to fly, but may have radio navigation equipment that permits operation in controlled airspace, with aids for letting-down to a major airport in bad weather and other items from modern technology that call for special training and skills. In short, the older aeroplane is essentially something that provides satisfaction to the pilot for the pleasure of pure flying, while the produce of recent years is a very practical travel tool for anyone who is qualified to use the resources that it is able to offer. The difference is as interesting as it is marked; but this writer knows which of the two switches him on!

Chapter 11
A Display Day

It is a summer Sunday; the clock on the tower of the Shuttleworth Agricultural College has just struck 8. Already the doors of Nos. 2 and 4 hangars are open, for this is the start of a day to be devoted to Service aeroplanes from 1910 onward. A handful of engineers and a pair of volunteer helpers are on the move with the Gladiator and the Tutor, whilst a couple of others are clearing the way to extract the LVG CV1 and Pup of World War I from their confined spaces in No. 2. The aerodrome is reasonably dry and the windsock is moving only gently, so conditions at this early hour seem well suited to a successful day's flying. Soon the home-based aeroplanes will be parked along the viewing enclosure fence to form the nucleus of the display flight line.

The first visitors are waiting patiently outside the aerodrome gates, each hoping to benefit from a crack-of-dawn start by obtaining a front row in the main viewing enclosure. One puts forward an excuse to be allowed in, showing a rather suspect press identity, but without a Shuttleworth press ticket or early pass he is asked to go back into the queue with the others. He feels that it was worth a try. Along the line of early stalwarts, the variety of brogues tells the true tale of enthusiasm for the happenings at Old Warden; a car load has driven overnight from Perth and another has just arrived from North Wales. Even more clearly apparent are the tongues from the far side of the Atlantic, for American aviation buffs (as they call themselves) just must come to see little old Shuttleworth. Of the English counties, Kent seems to generate a steady flow of early visitors, despite (or possibly because of?) the relative difficulty of the journey from the far side of London and the Thames. Before long, the first coach has joined the queue, for this is a fast-growing mode of travel to displays, with associations, societies and firms' social clubs coming en masse from all over Britain. Two binocular-laden cyclists have placed themselves in readiness to jump the car queue and to take full advantage of their space-saving manoeuvrability when the gates are opened.

Whilst this growing and welcome mass of expectant enthusiasm may be mentally singing "Why are we waiting?", the activity on the inside is growing in intensity. Car parkers are being briefed on the special requirements of the day; tickets and petty cash are being issued to the gate party; visiting stall-holders are preparing their wares for presentation to the public; Shuttleworth sales staff and programme sellers are making final arrangements to face the onslaught; a suspect drain is being checked and cleared to minimise the risk of trouble later in the day; and security arrangements are being finalised, with especial attention to the points of access to the airfield manoeuvring area. In an upstairs office the telephones ring incessantly.

Most of the essential participants in the overall scheme have started their duties that morning, for many are part-timers with other occupations, who devote these Sundays to the cause; the earlier preparatory arrangements have been carried out in the preceding days by members of the Collection's full-time staff. But on the operational side, preliminary plans for the day may have been been laid nearly a year previously; specific requests for demonstrations by Service aircraft must have been lodged with the Ministry of Defence by the first week in September of the previous year; the Civil Aviation Authority must have been notified several months before the event; the Airspace Utilisation Section of the National Air Traffic Service must have provided the required flight clearances; insurance, budgeting, publicity and other administrative angles must have been finalised long beforehand; and the detailed flying programme must have been prepared and circulated to all concerned in time for any problems to be raised, sorted and cleared well before the event.

The day itself shows little more than the tip of the organisational iceberg, but still many tasks remain, for some cannot be completed in advance. Perhaps the most significant of these is the effect of the weather on the programme, so fairly early in the morning the meteorological office at Honington, in Suffolk, provides the relevant information such as wind strengths and directions, cloud types, heights and amounts, whether icing is likely (it does not disappear in the summer), visibility (which, surprisingly, often does), whether rain is likely and details of the general situation; the concern extends not just around the Old Warden circuit, for aircraft are scheduled to appear on overhead slot times from as far apart as Royal Air Force, Lossiemouth in Morayshire and the Royal Naval Air Station at Culdrose in Cornwall. Unexpected winds or bad weather en route, even with perfect conditions at each end, can play tricks with the timings of overhead appearances.

On this occasion the forecast seems generally reasonable, with acceptable levels of cloud and visibility, but with one headache; the wind might increase in strength to 18 knots with gusts to 25. Forecast winds cannot always be precise and the overall trend can be affected by local variations, so this presents a planning problem that cannot be resolved until the allotted times at which the more wind-critical aircraft are due to perform. Almost certainly the Bristol Boxkite, scheduled in the show to represent the very beginning of military aviation, will be unable to fly; for safety, it will stay in its home in No. 1 hangar. The marginal cases, though, are outside already and the engineers are warned of the threatened wind so that they can prepare to tie them down; these include both the 1916 Sopwith Pup and the 1918 LVG CV1, each of which becomes difficult to manage in rough conditons. The decision to fly or not to fly is based not only on the strength of the wind, but also on its stability; a **steady** wind of 15 knots or so may be perfectly manageable, whereas a strength in single figures can produce blustery conditions and unacceptable vertical air movement. One of the display pilots has just air-tested the 1929 Hawker Tomtit and he reports that so far the wind is no problem; but it is too early to assess the likely state of play for the afternoon.

The gates are open and the early-morning enthusiasts have found their chosen parking and viewing spots. The initial queue has been cleared and only a few isolated visitors are coming in, for there is a noticeable gap between the 'dawn patrol' and the general run of spectators, many of whom endeavour to enter the aerodrome at the same time and then wonder why there are delays. Despite words of advice put over on press releases and in advertisements, advising people to come early, relatively few heed this and a fresh queue develops. The gate crews and car parkers work as hard as possible to keep everything and everyone moving, but only one or two individuals raising queries, or not having their money ready on arrival at the entrance, can generate lengthy tail-backs that become very difficult to clear. The senior

The Collection's 1918 Bristol Fighter and Avro 504 await their display turns,
unperturbed by the sudden arrival of the Red Arrows in their British Aerospace Hawks.

car parker walks to the main gate and states that the main
enclosures are nearly full and the overflow park on the opposite
side of the Biggleswade road must be brought into use when a
further 100 cars have been admitted. This changeover creates
temporary difficulties as people are needed to handle traffic and
occupants at both entry points at the same time; the switch from
one park to the other calls for a form of military precision.

Throughout this time visiting aircraft have been arriving from
all over Britain and the continent. Prior permission is required, as
on an occasion such as this the demand may exceed the supply;
the available parking area is limited and, to conform to both
Ministry of Defence and Civil Aviation Authority requirements,
adequate clearances must be maintained between the display line
(used by pilots as a positioning guide for their demonstrations)
and all obstructions. In this context a parked aeroplane or the
edge of the public viewing enclosure constitutes just such an
obstruction, so careful advanced planning includes a severe
restriction on the number of non-participating visiting aircraft
that can be allowed to land.

In addition to the spectators who come by air, several display aircraft are arriving. The Royal Navy's sole surviving Fairey Swordfish has plodded over from Yeovilton in Somerset; a Beaver of the Army Air Corps came on the previous day, but has just landed-back from a local reconnoitre of the display area; a private Harvard, flying in military markings by permission of the authorities, is marshalled into place alongside the only airworthy Avro Anson; this too is civil-owned, but still sports its Service serial, roundels and 'Royal Air Force Transport Command' on the fuselage upper decking. Authenticity is a keyword among those who take a serious view of aircraft preservation and the markings, lettering and colour schemes are very important.

Midday strikes. The commentator makes a few introductory announcements and reminds all display participants that they must attend the flying briefing at 12.30. This is a firm requirement and only in very rare circumstances can absence be accepted; in that case written and telephone instructions must have been given beforehand and agreed. Also over the public address comes a pleasant surprise: one of the Collection aircraft will fly for a

Old Warden aerodrome, with visitors departing shortly after one of the main flying displays.

179

height-judging competition and the winner will be granted a free flight. Many people beg for the chances to fly in these historic machines, but the airworthiness authorities rightly impose certain restrictions on the purposes for which they may be flown; namely demonstrations, ferry flights to and from displays and essentail air tests only. As exception has been negotiated, however, which allows free flights to be given in one of the more standard types on a maximum of four occasions in a year.

Briefing begins. The weather forecast is read and discussed. Clearly it is not possible yet to make firm decisions regarding some of the aircraft, so the final yes/no verdict will be agreed on the flight line; but with several participants due to appear on fixed overhead slot times, flexibility will be difficult to accommodate. As a result, several of the sequences are reshuffled to minimise the effect of last-minute flight cancellations and a revised version of the operational programme is issued. At this late stage any changes must be worked round the pre-agreed timings of visiting participants so that their slots remain unaffected.

Although most of the pilots present have performed at Old Warden on many occasions and all are experienced display performers, the basic rules of the game must be explained at every event. The Old Warden regulations are kept to a realistic minimum, based on several years of experience of the particular display site, but these include the golden oldies that no one may fly over or straight towards the crowds, the buildings or the parked aircraft. There are many positive guidelines regarding taxying paths, holding points whilst awaiting clearance to take-off, headings and positions of flypasts, the importance of keeping the operational area clear in case the pilot of a performing machine needs to land prematurely, sensitive areas that should not be overflown, action to take in the event of an engine being reluctant to start at the allotted minute and many others. Watches are checked and all are reminded of the need to keep to time. An early slippage of a minute can have repercussive effects throughout the display and could create an unacceptable hazard if a pilot on an overhead slot is unable to make radio contact before his initial run-in. All-round discipline plays a key role in the safety of any show and a participant who may wish to do anything unusual must ask and obtain permission during (not after!) the briefing, so that everyone likely to be affected (the controller, the marshallers, the next performer, the commentator et al) knows what to expect. Imagine the irretrievable delay if a

The visitors have gone home, but work continues for several hours. The Avro Triplane is wheeled to bed in No. 1 hangar at the end of a long day.

pilot of a non-radio aircraft completes his act and, instead of landing back at the allotted minute, flies straight on to return to his home base. No one is sure if he is flying away to build up speed or height for a final fast run-past and by the time that his intentions become self-explanatory, a minute or more has been lost. Hence the importance of briefing as the hard core of the day's programme. It is one of the numerous background activities that take place before, during and after the event to help to ensure that the display is smooth and enjoyable for those who have to come to see it — and, above all, that it is safe in all possible respects. A well-worn expression at Shuttleworth briefings is that whenever in doubt, safety must take precedence over spectacle.

Because of this need for safety and to ensure the minimum practical wear and tear on the historic aeroplanes, the pilots chosen to fly Shuttleworth aircraft in displays are vetted very carefully — and their subsequent performance is monitored throughout. Bad engine handling, undue stress on an airframe, opting to fly in conditions that should have dictated cancellation, or failure to request a wing-tip handler when taxying in windy conditions or in a confined space are among the signs that a person may not be quite to the standard expected. So pilots are selected not only for their abilities to fly accurately (important though this is) but because of their attitudes towards the responsibilities involved in being entrusted with some of the world's most valuable and irreplaceable historic aircraft. In short, airmanship in its broadest sense.

No rigid qualifications are laid-down for admission to the small band of selected Shuttleworth pilots. In addition to the importance of attitude and outlook, a varied flying background is essential. All have been trained in one of the Services and most are either current or former test pilots or flying instructors — or both. The numbers are kept to a practical minimum to ensure that each obtains some level of continuity. If an aeroplane flies only six times in a year, clearly it should be flown three times each by two pilots and not by six different people each having to undergo refamiliarisation for one annual sortie on the type. Training time is expensive in wear on engine and airframe components and must be restricted to flights that are unavoidable.

The show is scheduled to begin at 1400. A few minutes before this the controller is in radio contact with the RAF pilot of the Jaguar, who confirms that he is on target time and will come in low and fast at the allotted moment. He does. Some say that a new, noisy aircraft such as this is out of place among the rural scenery of Old Warden, but others like to see a comprehensive display covering both the ancient and the modern. In an attempt to satisfy both view points, two clearly defined patterns of display were introduced in 1982: all-embracing functions such as the one forming the basis of this chapter and old-style informal and unhurried 'flying occasions' devoted exclusively to the earlier eras of aviation.

On this occasion the programme is not geared to any particular historical order, but rather in terms of performance contrasts. Although the forecast wind caused several possible alterations to be planned, fortunately the local conditions stabilised nearly an hour before the show started and, on a fingers-crossed basis, the original and more purposeful sequence was reinstated. So as the Jaguar crosses the upwind boundary of the airfield on its final run, the LVG CV1, that slow but steady observation aircraft used by the Imperial German Air Force in 1918, receives a steady green light and lumbers slowly into the air. This gives viewers an instant reminder of the progress made in fewer than sixty years of aircraft development.

Many others follow. Each type has its band of supporters; some visitors may have flown or worked on machines that later became their favourites; later, because time makes memory into a very selective process. One may have been compelled to sweat for hours in very hot (or suffer in cold and wet) conditions trying to cure an ever-elusive snag when wanting to get away for a date, but these times of distress tend to fade compared with those magic moments when an aeroplane is all that it should be — and more. This, surely, must be part of the basis on which the growing interest in historic aeroplanes is built? Yet many of the keenest supporters have had no experience in flying, building or maintaining any machine. So what is the root of the attraction?

Whatever the cause, the next aeroplane in the programme can claim one of the biggest bands of followers: the Gloster Gladiator. Entering service in 1937 to become the RAF's last-

Energetic action by two engineers with their hands linked enables the Armstrong-Siddeley Mongoose engine of the 1929 Hawker Tomtit, K 1786, to burst to life. This was at an "away match" at a Royal Air Force display.

ever biplane fighter, the Gladiator appeals to almost everyone. Certainly it is an impressive performer and one that is in demand at displays away from Old Warden as well as at home; but as with all Shuttleworth aeroplanes, its flying must be severely rationed and normally it departs to distant places only four or five times in a year. This restriction accentuates the difference between 'home' and 'away' events, for only at Old Warden can visitors see a whole package of historic aircraft in one event in one afternoon.

The aim throughout is to present to visitors a show that flows smoothly from one item to the next. Sometimes an event runs as though on rails and little energetic conducting is required; yet, on another occasion, setbacks build-up from the beginning and every ounce of available energy and a clear head are needed to produce any form of worthwhile sequence. Obviously, known weather problems can be predictable hazards to success, but often there is no easily definable reason for an event running well or badly. It cannot be forecast; more surprisingly, the cause may not be clear even in a calm analytical rundown afterwards.

The show is running more successfully than was anticipated — so far; in this case, one leading reason is clear, for the threatened wind has not developed and there are no weather-related causes for cancellations or delays. The Magister, though, refused to start as promptly as it should, but the pilot began his preparations in good time and the decision about the sortie is taken sufficiently early to signal to the pilot of the Harvard to perform one act ahead of schedule. Even allowing for the essential engine-warming period, everything happens slickly and, at take-off, he is only 30 seconds behind the Magister's allotted time. The Harvard loses this amount from his performing slot and the show is back on schedule.

While this change was being conducted on the flight line, the controller had received a telephone call to warn him that the Spitfire G(B) from the Battle of Britain Memorial Flight had developed a slight coolant leak and would not be appearing. The Lancaster and Hurricane, however, were en route and a reorganised performance duration (15 minutes had been allotted for all three) could be agreed over the VHF radio with the formation leader in the Lancaster. A few words each way and agreement is reached for 12 minutes. Whilst nostalgia (and whatever the equivalent may be for the younger generations) worked overtime among the spectators, with the four synchronised Rolls-Royce Merlins of the Lancaster draining a little damp from the eyes of some of the hardiest on the field, a little more planning was under way with the home-based pilots. There were three extra minutes to be used, but only three, as after the next two aircraft the Seahawk would be on a fixed overhead slot and for fuel reserve reasons this could not be delayed. So it would not be practicable to add another aircraft into the avilable time and a compromise solution was agreed with the pilots concerned; each would add one minute to his sequence and, instead of starting to roll forward when the first machine was on the base leg of the circuit, the second would delay his take-off until the first had landed and cleared the runway. It worked well and there was no recognisable gap in the programme.

So the show proceeded. Although conditions were better than anticipated, local low-level turbulence was enough to keep the Boxkite indoors. However, visitors were not to be disappointed, for the programme closed with a performance by the Collection's 1937 Hawker Hind light bomber that had been restored over several years following a journey of 6,000 miles from Afghanistan. This large and powerful biplane and the crackle of its Rolls-Royce Kestrel engine combine to hold a steadily-increasing appeal to visitors. Not only is it the only Hind flying anywhere in the world, but it is the only airworthy example of the entire range of famous Hawker biplanes that formed the front-line mainstays of the Royal Air Force in the thirties.

The display is over, but activities are not. More than eighty visiting private aircraft are preparing to depart and for half-an-hour or so the usually quiet rural aerodrome becomes the busiest airfield in Britain. At one time twenty-three aicraft are counted in the take-off queue, but all get away smartly with guidance from the marshallers' bats and under the careful eye of the duty controller, who releases them by lamp signal at the shortest safe interval between machines. To ensure this smooth and rapid departure flow, regulations forbid any pilot to land back (except in emergency) for one hour after the end of the show.

Not only are aeroplanes leaving, but the road-borne crowds are winding their ways home. Many cannot resist the bumper-to-bumper conditions that must prevail immediately the flying demonstrations are finished, but some stay back for a while; for a picnic, a final walk round the exhibition hangars, a meal in the aerodrome restaurant, or just a final stare at the unique line-up of living examples of aviation's past. At the same time, though, those who made the afternoon possible are still busy closing down the day's affairs. The fire crew return the tender to its park and remove some of the specialist equipment to lock it away; the accountant and his helpers are assessing the results; flight sheets are being completed and any aircraft defects recorded; and when most visitors have left, still there are more than a dozen aeroplanes to wheel back to their beds.

The approach of dusk and an almost deserted grass aerodrome have an irresistible appeal. This is the time to fly, but everyone has worked extremely hard and most are exhausted, so any temptation that creates an extra load on anyone must be dismissed. Soon there will be a flying evening; then a few minutes in the air just before dusk can be enjoyed with a purpose. We must wait, and hope that plenty of visitors will arrive to imbibe the pleasures of such a unique occasion. A daytime display can be great value for participant and onlooker alike; but right at the end of a summer day there can be something even better! Also, an evening event seems to be more enjoyable to organise and to stage, ... so come along and share this special Shuttleworth experience.

Chapter 12
Old Warden Aerodrome

The grass aerodrome at Old Warden is almost an exhibit in its own right, for every possible effort has been made to retain a timeless atmosphere appropriate to the type of activity that takes place. Small all-grass aerodromes were commonplace from the start of flight until the forties, when many wartime elementary flying training schools fell into this category. Since then, they have become relative rarities, with the demands of modern aircraft dictating the length and strength of the available runways rather than the number of directions in which taking off and landing can be carried out. In the thirties, even the major scheduled airline services operated from omni-directional grass airports, but today nearly every such base has become just one long concrete or tarmac strip with no other areas maintained in safe, usable condition. A similar situation applies to many airfields used by the flying Services.

When Richard Shuttleworth obtained his first aeroplane — the Moth G-EBWD — the present site was not suitable to use and he flew from a nearby field on the family estate; but almost immediately he began to prepare his new aerodrome and to do so he needed to remove a number of trees. A story of the time is that his mother, who had no love for aeroplanes, tried very hard to dissuade him, so he encouraged her to take two holidays to the continent. While she was away he organised the felling of trees that would interfere with his flying activities and by the end of her second absence he had achieved his wish. Although apparently annoyed, Mrs. Shuttleworth is said to have recognised her son's independence of mind and his determination to fly, so from then on she supported his plans.

Although some sheds had been erected, the first real hangar to be built at Old Warden was the one nearest to the gate from the

Biggleswade road; this forms the basis of what is known today as No. 1 hangar. It was developed to include workshops and, later, rooms above, one of which became the drawing office. The stairs for this were made from a section of the main gangway from the Mauretania and these remain in use today. The second hangar was constructed during World War II, when the aerodrome was used as a civil-operated servicing base for light types then in military use. All the other hangars have been erected since the war.

During the Richard Shuttleworth era in the thirties, the small aerodrome, with a maximum available length of about 570 yards, had seen many light aircraft types and a number of engineering operations. One of the most unusual and certainly one of the larger types to appear briefly in 1933 was Blackburn Velos G-AAAW, with its 450 hp Napier Lion engine, a span of 48 feet and an all-up weight of 6,450 lbs. This rare beast, which was a trainer variant of the Blackburn Dart torpedo-bomber, was too thirsty a creature for private operation and soon was dismantled, to

The Blackburn Velos at Old Warden in 1934 shortly before is was dismantled. Many parts of its wooden airframe were used in rebuilding the 1909 Bleriot and 1910 Deperdussin monoplanes.

provide wood that was used later in restoration of the 1909 Bleriot and 1910 Deperdussin monoplanes.

In an attempt to improve performance and reduce the weight of the rugged Desoutter 1 monoplanes used by Heston-based Warden Aviation, G-AAPZ underwent major surgery at Old Warden. Instrumentation was improved, increased tankage fitted, wheel brakes incorporated and a modified MK11 tail unit installed, but the most drastic modification was replacement of the Cirrus Hermes engine by a Menasco C-4 Pirate. The results, though, were disappointing and subsequent tests proved that the American sales claims could not be matched in practice; the Pirate was unable to deliver its quoted power. Many years later, when other engines from the far side of the Atlantic were proved to be below par on performance, a court case in Britain resulted in a change in the way in which American engine capability and output were published, but the Shuttleworth Desoutter was the first in the line of test cases leading to this move; today the Desoutter languishes at Old Warden awaiting its eventual rebuild to fly again.

Reconditioned Percival Proctors of the Royal Air Force during World War II, in what is now No. 1 hangar.

In the fifties and early sixties there were no public displays staged at Old Warden. The aerodrome was not readily available for general use and in the main the only flying was the occasional test flight or ferry trip to or from a display elsewhere. In 1951 I had a lone first visit when I was asked to collect the 1932 Spartan Arrow G-ABWP which the Collection had sold for £100 to a private owner at White Waltham. I remember my surprise at the small amount of space available. Fifteen years passed before I saw it again and still there were many operating difficulties, for much of the space that had been used for flying during the war had been returned for agricultural use. Also, hay crops played a revenue-earning role, which for several weeks made taking-off or landing into an increasingly hazardous exercise as each new season matured.

Despite its long history the Collection was not opened to the general public on a regular basis until 1966, by which time the first Open Days had been established. Usually four or five aeroplanes would be flown before a crowd of a few hundred

Percival Proctors and North American Harvards at Old Warden during World War II.

people, with temporary rope-and-stake barriers erected for each occasion. These were very pleasant informal events, but during preceeding years many of the costs of maintaining the aircraft had been covered by covenanted donations from companies within the aircraft industry; now, however, these were ending and clearly some more positive plans were needed to ensure a survival into the seventies.

After the Collection had opened its gates to visitors every day, a shop was established; then a restaurant and snack bar (operated on a franchise basis) were introduced. On the aerodrome, though, much more happened. With such a small site, the management of the time was faced with decisions about how much of the field to keep available for aircraft operations and how much space could safely be made sterile as a car park and viewing enclosure. Maximum availability for flying was achieved by establishing two marked grass runways, but leaving a certain reserve of space for into-wind operation on days on which neither strip could be used safely by the oldest aeroplanes. The public enclosure was erected on a permanent basis, shaped so that the

The Avro 504K. Sopwith Pup, Blackburn, Deperdussin and Bleriot as stored in 1960 – before the collection was opened to the public every day. The Bristol Fighter stands in the foreground.

HRH The Prince of Wales is intrigued by the very basic cockpit layout of the 1910 Deperdussin.

boundaries of the viewing area were almost parallel to the two runways, providing the largest possible frontal area with almost a right-angle bend nearest to the centre of the airfield; this proved popular also with pilots, who could display the typically slow Shuttleworth aeroplanes to maximum effect round the outside of the bend.

Attendance at displays was increasing; and so were the costs of operating the Collection. The home-based historic aeroplanes formed the main base of attraction for visitors to the shows, for such sights could be seen nowhere else in the world, but to maintain series of events year after year, the organisers needed to inject some other attractions from further afield. Aircraft could appear on timed 'overhead slots' without landing, but the scope of a show could be extended considerably if some of the visting performers could present their aircraft on the airfield rather than just flying over.

So two main moves were made. For many years an area of ground to the east of the aerodrome had been isolated in the form of an island, bounded by streams on all sides. The surface was rough and the drainage even worse, but the Royal Engineers

The only pre-war hangar (now No. 1) in the mid-thirties.

welcomed the chance of a useful training exercise in re-routing a fast-flowing brook. The section alongside the existing boundary of the airfield was plugged with gravel to allow below-surface water movement to continue, whilst the eastern section was widened and deepened to accept the main stream. A contractor levelled and drained the area needed for a runway extension and a year later the north-west/south east strip was ready to accept a much wider range of aircraft types.

Although this extension vastly improved the usefulness of the airfield, the lengthening of one strip only generated a new problem, for with many aircraft types the crosswind limitations would mean that they could operate safely if the wind was close to the heading of the enlarged strip, but not otherwise. Imagine the dilemma of operating a timed display sequence with that background headache! So the next course of action was brought into play; the physical problem was minute compared with the earlier task, but the delays were greater. Although Shuttleworth property, predictably the land to the south-west of the other grass runway was declared to be the best piece of grazing ground in Bedfordshire. Such was the competition for space between the Trust's aviation and agricultural interests!

Clearly a solution could and would be found. A complicated compromise was agreed, involving occasional winter use of the airfield by the farm sheep, use of the off-runway airfield grass for crop (but not at hay height) and other well-argued points between the parties involved; but it was resolved amicably and eventually the necessary levelling, marking and fencing work was completed to extend the aerodrome to the South West. Unlike the other, longer strip, this runway was on level ground, with good clear approaches and climb-out paths at each end. This heading is used whenever possible on display days, for it offers good public viewing and is well-placed for access to the visiting aircraft parking areas. However, with so many wind-sensitive aeroplanes participating in an average Shuttleworth show, there are some days on which the north-west/south-east strip must become the active runway.

Today Old Warden aerodrome is physically hemmed-in to prevent much further extension of the total area. However, some ground to the east, near the windsock, remains available for draining and levelling; there is room along the line of hangars for

Richard Shuttleworth and Comper Swift at Old Warden. Hangars now occupy this site.

at least two more buildings to be erected in years to come; and, by arrangement with the Shuttleworth Agricultural College, the amount of off-airfield car parking space available is such that even on the busiest display days this has not been packed to its limits. More serious capacity limitatons are imposed by the narrow approach road (on which one of its two lanes must be kept clear for use by safety services) and the cramped feed-in point at the main gate. The former problem is insurmountable and any alteration to the latter would necessitate the loss of a small section of one runway and a corner of the aircraft parking/manoeuvring area.

Perhaps these small problems represent a form of disguised blessing, for the Shuttleworth Collection and Old Warden Aerodrome combine to make something that is so indescribably different. Many people have expressed their hope that the timeless atmosphere will be retained, that it will not be cheapened by overt commercialism, that the place will not grow into a large and impersonal entity lacking in traditional values. Considerable care has been taken throughout the development stages to ensure that the necessary expansion has been effected with as little

The first hangar shortly before completion in 1934, with an early production D.H. Leopard Moth.

change as possible to the overall 'air' that surrounds the Shuttleworth scene.

Clearly growth must bring some noticeable change. One that several visitors have not liked has been the increase in the scale of the flying functions, many of which have expanded from the casual open days of the sixties into full-scale, formal, but still unique flying displays. So in 1982 a fresh policy was introduced. A few major events were planned to cater for the needs of families and large crowds, while several small informal occasions were aimed at the more specialist visitors who sought space and freedom with opportunities for photography, filming and sound-recording. Three years previously the Collection had pioneered flying evenings, when some of the earliest of veteran aeroplanes could be demonstrated in the calm conditions that prevail so often in the last hour or two before dusk, but in 1982 the first flying afternoons were introduced to re-live some of the informal and unhurried atmosphere that had been one of the main features of the first open days. All concerned hope that this revised display

Richard Shuttleworth airborne in the Desoutter.

The Shuttleworth Collection

pattern can be continued for many years, therefore providing events to suit the needs and interests of every visitor.

Whatever happens elsewhere, Old Warden will remain as a small, all-grass aerodrome with a minimum of hard surface area, with pleasant rural surroundings, to provide almost a haven for those who wish to be surrounded by some of the best of the past. It is a popular place to visit, not only for those who arrive by road, but for many members of the private flying fraternity who seek somewhere to land that is away from the tarmac-surfaced, radio-cluttered airports and airfields that form the basis of the world of general aviation in the eighties. Because of this difference, Old Warden is a much-sought site for various non-Shuttleworth events such as model aeroplane competitions, kite festivals, fly-ins by aviation clubs and associations and occasionally private functions. On some occasions the aerodrome must be closed to all other aircraft, but each event helps to produce revenue for the Collection and on most days in the year the grass is available for all who wish to fly in to see the historic exhibits or just to relax in the open. Just in case something special is happening, though, prior permission is required and all pilots are asked to remember that Old Warden is a private, unlicensed airfield in a rural area where peace and quiet are appreciated by the Collection's neighbours!

Appendix I
Aircraft not on display

Although a guide of this nature must have an active life of several years, it would be unwise to include detailed reference to aircraft or other exhibits that are unlikely to appear on public display during this time. However, the Shuttleworth Collection owns a number of items that are undergoing very long-term restoration or are stored in various places awaiting their turns to enter the workshops. Brief details of the aeroplanes that fall into this group are given here:

B.A.T. Bantam: G-EACN. Built 1919. Service serial F 1654 and temporary civil registration K-123 (explained in Appendix II, page 203). A single-seat fighter built by the British Aerial Transport Company. Only 9 were produced due to the unreliability of the 170 hp ABC Wasp radial engine, but the type was raced regularly for a few years after Word War I. This specimen was stored for many years by Capt. C.P.B. Ogilvie at Primrose Garages, Watford, with the Collection's now-airworthy Bristol Fighter. Both were acquired together. The remains are in bad condition, but a volunteer enthusiast in Norfolk is attempting a complete rebuild.

ANEC II: G-EBJO. Built 1924. One of three monoplanes designed by W.S. Shackleton and constructed at Addlestone, in Surrey, by the Air Navigation and Engineering Company. Designed for an Air Ministry competition for 2-seaters; originally powered by an Anzani and later restored with a 32 hp Bristol Cherub. It had five owners, including Norman Jones of Tiger Club renown (1926) Allen Wheeler, a former Shuttleworth Aviation Trustee (1929) and Jimmy Edmunds who passed it to Richard Shuttleworth in 1937. It is a large machine for such low

Where do we begin? Components of the Hawker Hurricane I Z 7015 collected for checking against the inventory before serious restoration starts.

power, with a span of 38 feet and yet an empty weight of only 420 lbs. It has been stored at Old Warden since the start of World War II and is in need of a total rebuild.

Desoutter I: G-AAPZ. Constructor's No. D 25. Registered in 1931. A strut-braced high-wing monoplane produced at Croydon in 1930-31 but only slightly modified from the Dutch-designed Koolhoven FK 41. 41 were built, including 19 for National Flying Services. PZ had 2 owners before purchase in 1935 by Richard Shuttleworth, who replaced the Cirrus Hermes engine by a Menasco C-4 Pirate and completed several other modifications. It was exhibited statically at Hendon in 1951 and loaned to Torbay Air Museum in 1971. Now stored at Old Warden; it is scheduled for eventual restoration.

Southern Martlet: G-AAYX. A single-seat biplane developed from the Avro Baby, the Martlet went into limited production at Shoreham between 1930 and 1931, following a prototype that first flew in August 1929. Variously the ABC Hornet, Armstrong-Siddeley Genet and upright de Havilland Gipsy were used for power. Shortly after World War II, this sole survivor was owned and operated by Butlins to give displays to holidaymakers at Pwllheli. It is stored at Old Warden awaiting restoration and is in need of many parts for its Genet engine. It is an attractive little aeroplane and will be an added bonus to the flight line when the time comes.

Hawker Hurricane I: Z 7015. Build by the Canadian Car and Foundry Co. and later converted in Britain to a Sea Hurricane I B for catapult operation from merchant ships for convoy protection. After the war, it was used as a ground instructional airframe at Loughborough (see Spitfire Vc) before transfer to the Shuttleworth Collection. Used statically in the film 'The Battle of Britain' before partial restoration at Staverton by a volunteer team, then stored at Old Warden for several years before transfer to Duxford in 1981 for the start of a long and very extensive rebuild. Later it will become an active flying partner for the Collection's airworthy Spitfire.

Supermarine Spitfire XI: PL 963. An unarmed high-level photographic reconnaissance version of the Spitfire fighter. Used in World War II as a personal "hack" by the U.S. Air Attaché in Britain; later it was passed to the Collection by Vickers - Armstrong and flown in to Old Warden. Following display as a gate guardian for several years, it was dismantled and stored inside to avoid deterioration and then taken to Duxford where a volunteer crew is undertaking a major rebuild. For more Spitfire information, see Chapter 5 page 101.

Avro Anson 19/2: TX 183. Built for the RAF in 1947 as an Anson C 19 Series 1 with wooden wings and converted to a series 2 in the early fifties. It is a standard communications aircraft and served with the Aircraft and Armaments Experimental Establishment at Boscombe Down; on retirement it was purchased by the Collection in 1967 and flown into Old Warden by an RAF crew. It was exhibited outdoors for several years during which time it was available for visitors to walk around inside, but following deterioration, it was moved to Duxford to be hangared. Long-term restoration is being carried out there by a volunteer crew. For an explanation of Anson dates, see page 203 of Appendix 1.

The 1924 ANEC II at Old Warden in the mid-thirties; currently it awaits a complete rebuild.

Percival jet Provost T.1: G-AOBU. Logical successor to the piston Provost (see Chapter 5, page 105) and precursor of today's RAF basic trainer. Only 10 Mark 1s were built for Service trials, but this specimen was used by the makers and appeared at the 1955 SBAC Display at Farnborough. It is on long loan from the Collection to Loughborough University for use as an instructional airframe and is unlikely to be restored as part of the Shuttleworth flying fleet.

In addition to these historic aircraft that are not on view at Old Warden, a reproduction 1916 **Sopwith Triplane** is being built for the Collection by Northern Aeroplane Workshops, an all-volunteer group in Yorkshire. Now under construction to original Sopwith works drawings, with Sir Thomas Sopwith's personal approval, it is to be powered by an original 130 hp Clerget rotary engine now being built-up from two specimens held at Old Warden for many years. This aeroplane will join the flying fleet and will graduate to a full page in future editions of the guide.

Appendix II
Markings, Colour Schemes and Dates of Origin

Where praticable, the aeroplanes in the Shuttleworth Collection are presented in colours and markings that are appropriate to their eras. This brief general description, therefore, may be helpful towards understanding the many variations.

Early Flying Machines: These were finished in a clear dope only to tauten the fabric; colours were not used because of the extra weight. No formal registration markings were carried, but today the survivors have new national identities recorded by the British Aircraft Preservation Council, eg the Collection's 1910 Deperdussin is listed as BAPC 4.

Military aeroplanes: Aircraft were painted in schemes appropriate to their intended duties and areas of operation. In peacetime conditions, a silver finish (natural or painted) has been a standard practice, with, for example, yellow (later dayglo orange) conspicuity-bands on wings and round the rear of fuselages on machines used for training. At some periods, eg in the mid thirties and just after World War II, many trainers were painted yellow overall, sometimes, in the first case, with polished silver engine cowlings.

In wartime or with the threat of war, aircraft have been painted in dark colours, such as olive drab in the 1914-18 period; or the lozenge camouflage used by the Germans, which can be seen on the Collection's LVG CVI; World War II saw many schemes, including dark earth and green as a standard camouflage, replaced in some areas by grey and green. For desert operations a lighter sandy brown has been used, while a deepish blue has been standard on many high-altitude photographic reconnaissance aircraft since the early forties.

Although there have been certain exceptions, often for security reasons, generally the serial numbers of Service aeroplanes have been a guide to their age, with consecutive numbers issued for specific production batches. Starting with A1 in 1916, a single letter followed by up to four figures was used until the early part of World War II, by which time all these had been allotted; as an example, K and L prefixes were standard during the thirties, such as L8032 of the Shuttleworth Gladiator of 1938. When two-letter prefixes became necessary, the numbers were reduced to three, eg AR 501, which is the Collection's 1941 Spitfire.

Civil Aeroplanes: Colours are largely a matter of owners' personal choices, with private machines painted to individual taste and commercial aircraft to the operators' house schemes. For practicable purposes, as far as surviving machines are concerned, (although a temporary scheme from May to July 1919 used the letter K followed by three figures from 100 onwards) all British civil aircraft have a five-letter registration, comprising a G followed by a dash and four letters giving the individual identity. Aircraft registered between July 1919 and 1928 have G-E prefixes (E standing for England, with C used for Canada etc), but in 1928 this was abandoned by international agreement and the countries in the then British Empire acquired their own lettering. Machines registered in Britain started again at the beginning of the alphabet, i.e. G-AAAA. Examples of both schemes can found in the Collection, such as the 1928 DH6OX Moth G-EBWD and the 1935 Percival Gull G-ADPR. Today G-B ... registrations are issued, but now the Civil Aviation Authority will issue out-of-sequence allocations to those who ask, making impossible the task of using the letters as a guide to a machine's year of registration.

Dates of origin: If there is one aspect in the search for historical accuracy that guarantees a headache for an author, the date to quote for a type must take a lead! What is the correct date to use? The year in which design work started or finished, the year in which the prototype (which may have been very different from the later production machine) flew, the time of the type entering service, the year in which the particular mark or variant was introduced or the date on which the exhibit was built?

The Avro Anson provides a typically confusing example: the Avro 652 was a small civil airliner designed in 1934 for Imperial Airways and delivered in March 1935; the Avro 652A was a military derivative subsequently named Anson, which entered R.A.F. squadron service in March 1936; the civil Avro Nineteen, still with type designation of Avro 652A, started from a physical conversion of an R.A.F. Anson 12 and flew in this form in 1945; from this grew the military Anson 19, produced in quantity in 1946 and 1947, and the Collection's specimen is from the first production batch of this mark; but this is not the end of the tale, for TX 183 was built as an Anson 19 series 1 with the original-style wooden wing and, in common with all others then in service, these were changed to the tapered metal wings in the late fifties to become an Anson 19 series 2 but still designated Avro 652A! That is what the machine is now, but as it was built in 1946 we have used that date in this guide. This seems to be the most honest course of action!

Consider also the Gloster Gladiator; the private-venture prototype Gloster S5.37 flew in September 1934, but was unnamed until the R.A.F. placed an order in July of the following year. The type entered squadron service in February 1937. The Collection's specimen is built-up from two different, but original, airframes. Although in 1934 there was an aeroplane in existence that today would be called Gladiator, at the time there was no aeroplane with that name, so 1939 seems the year to use.

As a general base, the years used are those in which the standard production versions entered military or civil service, but still there are problems. Design work on the little amateur-built Granger Archaeopteryx began in 1926 and it first flew in 1930, but its identity G-ABXL dates it as 1932, for it was not registered until that year. Only one was constructed, so there cannot be a time of entering service and in this case reference to the year of the first flight gives due credit to the foresight of its designers.

What about the Spitfire? The prototype flew in 1936 and the first Mark 1s were delivered to the R.A.F. in 1938; but the Collection's specimens are a mark Vc of 1941 and a photographic reconnaissance mark XI of the following year, so the dates appropriate to the marks (which in fact are the years in which the individual aircraft were built) have been used.

The first Bristol Fighter flew in 1916 and the type went into action in 1917, but the Collection's specimen was not built until the end of the war — in late 1918. However, as it is a standard production machine as built in quantity in the earlier year, commonsense seems to say that 'Bristol Fighter 1917' is the most appropriate description.

There are many other anomalies. The problems of dating are as endless as the choices, so perhaps you will accept that while the results in this book may be open to question, they are as accurate as history allows?

* * *

Registrations allocated by the Civil Aviation Authority to aircraft that do not display their civil identities:

Registration	Type	Identity or Marks Displayed (if any)
G-ASPP	Bristol Boxkite	—
G-AWII	Supermarine Spitfire	AR501
G-ANKT	DH-82A Tiger Moth	T6818
G-AOTD	DHC-1 Chipmunk	WB588
G-ARSG	Avro Triplane	"Avro"
G-EBNV	English Electric Wren	"4"
G-AEPH	Bristol F-2B	D8096
G-AANI	Blackburn Monoplane	—
G-AANJ	LVG-CVI	7198/18
G-EBIA	SE-5A	F904
G-ACNB	Avro 504K	E3404
G-AWRY	Percival Provost	XF836
G-AJRS	Miles M14A Magister	P6382
G-AENP	Hawker Hind	41H 81902
G-AHSA	Avro Tutor	K3215
G-AFTA	Hawker Tomtit	K1786
G-AANH	Deperdussin Monoplane	—
G-AMRK	Gloster Gladiator	L8032
G-AANG	Bleriot Monoplane	—
G-EBKY	Sopwith Pup	N5180

Appendix III— Comparative Summary of Technical Details

Aircraft	Year	Engine, No. of cylinders, layout (see ii) & h.p.	Span (ft. & ins.)	Tare Weight (lbs.)	Max. Speed (mph)	Identification, equipment & remarks. (F) indicates fixed forward-firing gun.
Bleriot XI	1909	Anzani (v)-3-25	28	484	40	C/N 14 (BAPC 3)
Deperdussin	1910	Anzani (y)-3-35	28 9	617	55	C/N 43 not confirmed (BAPC-4)
Blackburn	1912	Gnome (R) 7-50	38	1050	60	C/N 7 (BAPC 5)
Bristol Boxkite	1910 *	see iii	35	835	45	Reproduction (BAPC 2)
Avro Triplane IV	1910 *	see iii	32	650	48	Reproduction (BAPC 1)
Avro 504K	1918*	le Rhone (R) -9-110	36	1250	82	E3404 (not original serial) Built as H 5199
Sopwith Pup	1916	le Rhone (R) -9-80	26 6	780	105	N5180 (G-EBKY) 1 Vickers (F)
Bristol F. 2b	1917	Falcon (v)-12-275	39 4	1900	110	D 8096 (G-AEPH). 1 Vickers (F); 1 Lewis
RAF S.E.5a	1917	Viper (v)-8-200	26 7½	1530	132	F904 (G-EBIA) 1 Vickers (F); 1 Lewis (F)
L.V.G. C.VI	1917	Benz (u)-6-230	44 8	2090	110	7198/18, c/n 4503. 1 Spandau (F) 1 Parabellum
E.E. Wren	1923	ABC (h)-2-4	37	232	48	CN 4 (BAPC 11)
D.H. 53	1923	Scorpion (h)-2-35	30	370	70	G-EBHX
D.H. 51	1924	Airdisco (v)-8-120	37	1340	98	G-EBIR (VP-KAA)
D.H. 60x Moth	1928	Cirrus Hermes (u)-4-105	30	930	102	G-EBWD
Hawker Tomtit	1928	Mongoose (r)-5-150	28 6	1100	124	K1786 (G-AFTA)
Parnall Elf	1929	Cirrus Hermes (u)-4-105	31 2	1140	112	G-AAIN
D.H. 60G Moth	1930	Gipsy 1 (u)-4-100	30	920	120	G-ABAG
D.H. 80a Puss Moth	1930	Gipsy Major (i)-4-130	36 9	1265	128	G-AEOA. Loaned to the Collection

	Year	Engine				
Avro Tutor	1930	Lynx (r)-7-215	34	1800	122	K3215 (G-AHSA)
Granger Archaeopteryx	1930	Cherub (h)-2-34	30	450	90	G-ABXL
Desoutter	1930	Menasco Pirate (i)-4-130	36	1180	115	G-AAPZ Awaiting restoration
D.H. 82a Tiger Moth	1932	Gipsy Major (i)-4-130	29 4	1115	109	T 6818 (G-ANKT)
D.H. 83 Fox Moth	1932	Gipsy Major (i)-4-130	30 10½	1100	113	G-CEJ Loaned to the Collection
Ceirva C30a	1934	Genet Major (r)-7-140	37	1200	100	K 4235 (G-AHMJ). Not airworthy.
Mignet 'Flying Flea'	1934	Cherub (h)-2-34	20	225	65	G-AEBB
D.H. 88 Comet	1934	2x Gipsy Six R (i)-6-230	44	2840	237	G-ACSS (K 5084) Being restored.
Percival Gull-Six	1935*	Gipsy Six (i)-6-185	36 2	1500	175	G-ADPR (AX866)
B.A. Swallow	1935	Niagara (r)-5-95	42 8½	990	104	G-AFCL Loaned to the Collection
D.H. 94 Moth Minor	1937	Gipsy Minor (i)-4-92	36 7	960	118	G-AFNG Loaned to the Collection
Hawker Hind	1934*	Kestrel (v)-12-640	37 3	3250	186	ex Royal Afghan Air Force, 1 Vickers (f), 1 Lewis
Gloster Gladiator	1934	Mercury (r)-9-840	32 3	3450	253	L 8032 (G-AMRK) 4 Browning (F)
Miles Magister	1937	Gipsy Major (i)-4-130	33 10	1286	135	P 6382 (wrongly G-AJDR)
Hawker Hurricane I	1937	Merlin (v)-12-1030	40	4670	316	Z 7015 8 Browning (F). Being restored at Duxford.
Supermarine Spitfire Vc	1941*	Merlin (v)-12-1440	36 10	4800	374	AR 501 (G-AWII) 2 x 20 mm cannon plus 4 Browning (F)
Avro Anson 19	1946 *	2 x Cheetah (r)-7-420	57 6	7400	190	TX 183. At Duxford. Being restored.
DHC-1 Chipmunk	1946	Gipsy Major (i)-4-145	34 4	1417	138	WB 588 (G-AOTD)
Percival Provost	1951	Leonides (r)-9-550	35 2	3350	190	XF 836

N.B.

(i) In most cases dates given are those of first flights, unless either changes are made or long delays occur before a type goes into production, when the year of entering service is quoted. * indicates that earlier versions flew before the year given.

(ii) Engines quoted are those fitted to Shuttleworth aircraft, although in many cases other types were used also. Engine layouts are: (R) Rotary: (r) static radial; (u) upright inline; (i) inverted inline; (v) vee; (h) horizontally opposed.

(iii) The Boxkite and Triplane are reproductions fitted with 90 h.p. Continental and 75 h.p. Cirrus engines. Originals had 50 or 70 h.p. Gnome or 35 h.p. Green respectively.

(iv) Dimensions, weights and performance figures are quoted from specifications or, in some cases, from actual measurements, weights or recorded speeds of Shuttleworth machines.

(v) There are several other historic aeroplanes owned by or loaned to the Collection, but these await long-term restoration. They include the 1919 BAT Bantam, 1924 ANEC and 1929 Southern Martlet.

Appendix IV
Information for Visitors

Location:
The Shuttleworth Collection is housed at Old Warden Aerodrome, which is 2 miles west of the A1 trunk road near Biggleswade in Bedfordshire. The nearest railway station is Biggleswade, on the Eastern Region, while access is possible also from Bedford on the Midland Region, as an occasional United Counties bus service operates between the two stations and passes close to the aerodrome.

Opening:
Except for a week at Christmas, the Collection is open to visitors daily from 10 am until 5 pm, or dusk if this is earlier. A gift shop is open at the same times and a restaurant and snack bar are operated by a contractor on a concession basis. There is ample space for picnics in pleasant rural surroundings.

Education facilities:
Facilities are available for parties to be given introductory talks or guided tours; a special leaflet gives details. Advance bookings must be made.

The Collection publishes a number of books and booklets dealing with various types of exhibits. A companion volume to this guide, 'From Bleriot to Spitfire', describes the handling qualities of many of the historic aeroplanes.

There is a limited library and research facility, for which a charge is made to users. A small lecture room may be hired by approved organisations.

Lectures on the Collection or on specific aspects of the Collection's activities, e.g. restoration, flying or displays, are available to recognised bodies, but requests should be made in writing well in advance of any chosen dates.

Displays:

Flying displays are held regularly between April and October each year and on some occasions the historic vehicles are paraded. Also, functions such as model aircraft competitions and kite festivals take place each summer. A calendar of each season's events is available free of charge on receipt of a stamped, addressed envelope. Normally this is published in March.

Charitable status:

The Richard Ormonde Shuttleworth Remembrance Trust is a registered charity number T146972-105. Donations should be made payable to the Shuttleworth Collection. Where appropriate, gifts by Deed of Covenant enable the Collection to recover the income tax paid by the donor.

The Swiss Garden:

An attractive garden with ponds, paths and bridges is owned by the Richard Ormonde Shuttleworth Remembrance Trust, but is leased to Bedfordshire County Council. It adjoins the aerodrome.

Old Warden Aerodrome:

Old Warden is a small, private, unlicensed grass aerodrome. Visitors are welcome to fly in subject to obtaining prior permission. It is in a quiet farming area and pilots are asked to avoid low flying or any other inconsiderate activity that may disturb the peace of the neighbourhood.

Support:

The Shuttleworth Veteran Aeroplane Society serves as a supporting body to the Collection. New members are welcome and details are available on request.

Accuracy:

All information in this book is considered to be accurate at the time of publication in the Summer of 1982, but neither the Trust nor the Collection can be responsible for any changes that may occur during its period of validity as a guide.

Information:

The address for all communications is the Shuttleworth Collection, Old Warden Aerodrome, Biggleswade, Bedfordshire SG18 9ER. The telephone number is 076 727 288.

Index